Developing Iraq's Security Sector

The Coalition Provisional Authority's Experience

Andrew Rathmell, Olga Oliker, Terrence K. Kelly,
David Brannan, Keith Crane

Prepared for the Office of the Secretary of Defense
Approved for public release; distribution unlimited

 NATIONAL DEFENSE RESEARCH INSTITUTE

The research described in this report was prepared for the Office of the Secretary of Defense (OSD). The research was conducted in the RAND National Defense Research Institute, a federally funded research and development center sponsored by the Office of the Secretary of Defense, the Joint Staff, the Unified Combatant Commands, the Department of the Navy, the Marine Corps, the defense agencies, and the defense Intelligence Community under Contract DASW01-01-C-0004.

Library of Congress Cataloging-in-Publication Data

Developing Iraq's security sector : the Coalition Provisional Authority's experience / Andrew Rathmell ... [et al.].
    p. cm.
    "MG-365."
    Includes bibliographical references.
    ISBN 0-8330-3823-0 (pbk. : alk. paper)
    1. Civil defense—Iraq. 2. National security—Iraq. 3. Law enforcement—Iraq.
4. Police—Iraq. I. Rathmell, Andrew.

UA929.I67D48 2005
355.4'9—dc22

2005017760

Cover photo courtesy Reuters/Landov. Mohammed Jalil, photographer.

The RAND Corporation is a nonprofit research organization providing objective analysis and effective solutions that address the challenges facing the public and private sectors around the world. RAND's publications do not necessarily reflect the opinions of its research clients and sponsors.

RAND® is a registered trademark.

Published 2005 by the RAND Corporation
1776 Main Street, P.O. Box 2138, Santa Monica, CA 90407-2138
1200 South Hayes Street, Arlington, VA 22202-5050
201 North Craig Street, Suite 202, Pittsburgh, PA 15213-1516
RAND URL: http://www.rand.org/
To order RAND documents or to obtain additional information, contact
Distribution Services: Telephone: (310) 451-7002;
Fax: (310) 451-6915; Email: order@rand.org

Preface

This report is the concluding part of the RAND Corporation's support contract with the Coalition Provisional Authority (CPA), under which RAND was tasked to provide analyses on important policy issues. Because of the CPA's dissolution on June 28, 2004, this report is provided to its successor organization, the U.S. Mission in Baghdad. This report will be of interest to U.S. and other government personnel who are now engaged in making policy on Iraqi security and in supporting the development of the Iraqi security sector.

This research was conducted within the International Security and Defense Policy (ISDP) Center of the RAND National Defense Research Institute, a federally funded research and development center sponsored by the Office of the Secretary of Defense, the Joint Staff, the unified combatant commands, the Department of the Navy, the Marine Corps, the defense agencies, and the defense Intelligence Community.

For more information on RAND's ISDP Center, contact the director, James Dobbins. He can be reached by email at james_dobbins@rand.org; by phone at 703-413-1100, extension 5134; or by mail at RAND Corporation, 1200 South Hayes Street, Arlington, VA 22202-5050. More information about RAND is available at www.rand.org.

Contents

Figures and Tables

Figures

Tables

Summary

Soon after the coalition's occupation of Iraq began in April 2003, it became evident that prewar assumptions about the security situation that would follow the ouster of Saddam Hussein had been unduly optimistic. The environment was not benign—in fact, it was deteriorating. Iraqi security forces had largely disintegrated, and those that remained were incapable of responding to rising criminality and political violence. In this environment, the coalition confronted three security imperatives: (1) to restore order and neutralize insurgents and terrorists; (2) to rebuild Iraqi security forces, which could eventually take on responsibility for Iraq's security; and (3) to build security sector institutions, such as national security management institutions, the interior and defense ministries, and the justice sector, to ensure that the Iraqi security sector could be an effective bulwark for a democratic Iraq in the future.

At the time that the Coalition Provisional Authority (CPA) handed over authority to the Iraqi Interim Government (IIG) on June 28, 2004, it was clear that the coalition had made little progress in the first task. Insurgent and terrorist violence was escalating, organized crime was flourishing, and the security situation was threatening both the political transition and the reconstruction program. The coalition's record on the second and third tasks, however, is somewhat less simply categorized. From April 2003, the coalition embarked on efforts to rapidly field Iraqi security forces and to build security sector institutions. This effort was broad in scope, but its implementation was patchy, its results were varying, and its ultimate success or failure remains difficult to determine.

Significant analysis has focused on the inability of the coalition to adequately counter political violence and crime in post-Saddam Iraq. There has also been considerable discussion about the coalition's effort to develop Iraqi security forces. The matter of institution-building, however, has been largely ignored by observers and policy-makers; it is often seen as a long-term issue that is too far removed from immediate security needs. But the three efforts are interdepend-ent: Iraq's future security depends on its indigenous security forces, and these forces' success and sustainability depend on the institutions that support them. This report concerns itself with the efforts to build both forces and institutions in Iraq. It provides a historical record of the coalition's experience and seeks, insofar as is possible at this early stage, to draw lessons from the successes and failures of that experience.

Invalid Assumptions

Coalition prewar planning had assumed a benign security environ-ment and an Iraqi police force able to maintain order. A limited amount of preparation had been undertaken to provide advisory teams to reform the Iraqi security ministries and forces, but a large-scale program to restructure and rebuild them was not envisaged. When prewar assumptions proved invalid in the course of 2003, the coalition struggled both to maintain order and to improvise plans for the reconstruction and reform of Iraq's security sector.

In the face of growing and multiple insurgencies, these plans increasingly focused on rapidly training and fielding Iraqi forces. Institutional development proceeded in parallel but as less of a prior-ity. When the November 15, 2003, agreement shortened the CPA's timeline, setting a dissolution date at the end of June 2004, the coali-tion began to focus much more on building Iraqi capacity for self-governance. However, programmatic delays combined with the very short time horizon hampered the implementation of the capacity-building, reform, and institution-building programs.

The Security Sector at Transition—and Beyond

It is not surprising that, at the end of June 2004, when the IIG took power, the Iraqi security sector was unable to guarantee basic public safety, let alone enforce the rule of law. Nor should it come as a surprise that this remains the case in early 2005, at the time of this writing. Whether assessed in terms of numbers of trained personnel, deployment of equipment, creation of infrastructure, unit operational capability, institutional development, command and control mechanisms, or governance arrangements, the reconstruction and reform program is clearly still in its early stages. This can be seen in the following seven key elements of Iraq's security sector.

Iraqi National Security Institutions

Despite a late start, there was actually significant progress in this area, perhaps in part because it was considerably less labor intensive than several others. The CPA had, by June 2004, helped Iraq's political leaders to establish national security institutions, most notably a Ministerial Committee on National Security (MCNS). This committee had engaged in policymaking and strategy development, and its supporting institutions had begun to be built. The committee was continued under the IIG by Prime Minister Iyad Allawi. However, there is little sign yet of the development of true coordination between ministries at working levels, facilitated by a national security advisory staff. The reversion to hierarchical, patronage-based stovepipes is a real danger in Iraq, which, if it occurs, would reduce the quality of national security policymaking.

The Defense Sector

The effort to create a defense ministry from scratch in less than half a year was, from the beginning, recognized to be likely to produce a partial solution. The effort focused on identifying appropriate personnel at a variety of levels. This decision may serve Iraq well if the new Ministry of Defense (MoD) is permitted to mature into a well-established organization. However, the failure to institutionalize key reform processes in the MoD, evidenced by the speed with which some of the personnel were bypassed upon the departure of the CPA, makes it uncertain whether this maturity will be achieved. The institutional weaknesses of the MoD are a particular problem because the Iraqi Armed Forces are developing rapidly. While this is important to meet immediate security requirements, it poses two serious risks: (1) that the armed forces will grow rapidly into a powerful institution, only nominally governed by a weak civilian ministry, or (2) that they will become primarily an internal security force, rivaling a range of other internal security actors.

The Interior Ministry
When the CPA formally abolished all the other Iraqi security institutions, the Iraqi Police Service (IPS) was thrust into the front line of both public safety and counterinsurgency. This was a mission for which it was not postured, trained, or equipped. Under Saddam, the police had a secondary status; all serious internal security tasks were handled by other security and paramilitary entities. Not only did the coalition expect the police to move from being a neglected, secondary player to being a professional police force, it encouraged the police to do so in the face of an extreme level of violence that no democratic police force in the world would have likely been able to face.

Against this background, by July 2004, the police recruiting, training, equipping, and infrastructure development programs were making progress, compared with their abysmal state early in the occupation. These improvements have largely continued. With the continued injection of foreign funds, equipment, advisors, and military support, the police and border forces are likely to develop considerable capability by mid-2006. However, delays in particular programs, such as the police communications network and national identification systems, are likely to constrain the effectiveness of these forces considerably.

Furthermore, there remain serious concerns in two areas. First is the ability of the IPS to deal with political violence and with serious, well-armed insurgents and organized criminals, efforts that may admittedly be beyond the scope of any police force. This creates a requirement for specialized internal security units and leads to the continued domestic use of MoD troops. Second is the slow pace of institutional development in the interior ministry. This creates concerns about the long-term governance structures and democratic accountability of Iraq's internal security forces.

Infrastructure Security

The bulk of the infrastructure security forces, the Facilities Protection Service, is, by design, minimally trained and has limited functions. However, such critical ministries as oil and electricity are deploying increasingly professional security forces that are helping to make their infrastructure more resilient. An important outstanding issue to be dealt with is the regulation of private security firms and the ability of the state to dispense with the services of tribal guards. The legal framework regulating such structures is not being effectively enforced, and semiprivatized guard forces continue to proliferate.

The Justice Sector

Considerable progress was made in judicial reform between April 2003 and the end of June 2004, with the completion of a process to vet all sitting judges and the passage of legislation to create an independent judiciary. This progress, however, was in spite of the fact that this sector never received the support it deserved. A long-term program of institutional development and training across the rule-of-law continuum was not developed by the coalition during the occupation and is only now being defined. It is also vital that combined judicial and law enforcement institutions be developed, ones that are able to confidently tackle organized and violent crime. The wider anticorruption effort, meanwhile, was pursued in a piecemeal manner; there is no certainty that the measures taken will succeed. Furthermore, bringing Iraq's prisons up to a humane standard will take many years of intensive commitment by Iraqi and international bodies.

The Intelligence Services

The failure to develop an integrated, coordinated Iraqi intelligence apparatus ranks as an important CPA failure. Although there was initial reluctance within the CPA to work on intelligence reform, given the terrible record of Iraq's intelligence services in the past, it should have become quickly evident that an Iraqi-owned, democratically accountable intelligence capability coordinated across the security sector would be critical to the success of both the counterinsurgency campaign and the fight against organized crime. Iraqi intelligence capacity was instead developed in a stovepiped and uncoordinated manner.

Disarmament, Demobilization, and Reintegration (DDR)

A formal DDR process was not appropriate in Iraq, since the armed forces had self-demobilized. It is clear that the loss of status among former officers, the lack of jobs, and a plentiful supply of weaponry have been factors in fueling the insurgency. The coalition addressed these concerns with a stipend program and the appointment of "clean" former officers to the security forces and ministries. The lesson may be that, while demobilization was unnecessary and disarmament perhaps unfeasible, more resources should have been devoted to reintegration from the start of the occupation.

In relation to militias, the late start and limited staff and budget applied to the transition and reintegration (TR) process made success unlikely from the start, even if the political circumstances had been more propitious. From February through June 2004, significant progress was made, but without ongoing support from either the IIG or the coalition nations, the TR effort was doomed to languish.

Assessing Progress

Based on a threefold model of progress in security sector reform that includes change at the level of individuals, institutions, and integrative tendencies, we can make some tentative, qualitative generalizations as to how much progress was made in the Iraqi security sector.

At the level of individuals, the coalition did make a major effort to remove Saddam-era officers and senior officials steeped in the abusive and corrupt ways of the old regime. These individuals would otherwise have been a brake on reform, as has indeed happened in the interior ministry, where many Saddam-era personnel remained in place. The coalition also had some success in informing Iraqi political leaders and senior officials about the principles of good security sector governance.

The bulk of the coalition's reform work concentrated on building effective security sector institutions, notably the ministries. The primary focus was on building their managerial and administrative capacity, but efforts were also made to inculcate reformed practices. There is a striking difference, for instance, between the defense ministry—rebuilt from scratch along U.S.-UK lines—and the interior ministry, which has been only marginally touched by reform efforts. Institutional reform has therefore been patchy but in any case is a very long-term process that will only succeed if future Iraqi leaderships champion the cause.

Integration across the security sector and with the wider society is also a mixed story. The MCNS and to some extent local-level joint coordination centers were partial success stories. The coalition, however, failed to overcome the rigid ministerial compartmentalization inherited from Saddam. As for wider integration with society, the CPA and its successor Iraqi government did make some progress in reorienting the security sector into one that services society rather than one that preys on it.

Thus, although the security sector capacity-building and reform program was behind in many of its targets, in the longer view it was moving in the right direction and laying the foundations of what is likely to remain for some years a tremendously ambitious reconstruction and reform program.

Underlying Problems and Lessons

This report identifies six problems underlying the coalition's approach to the Iraqi security sector that the authors believe lie at the core of the failures identified. These problems are also broader lessons for security sector reform (SSR) programs in Iraq and elsewhere.

1. **A lack of worst-case and contingency planning.** Both in the run-up to the war and during the occupation, there was a failure to conduct worst-case (or even other-case) analysis. This meant that coalition planners were unable to prepare effectively even for expected contingencies or failures. In regard to the security sector, this led, for example, to a failure to prepare for the infiltration and intimidation of police forces, which forced coalition troops to step back into the front line of security in key urban areas.

2. **Structural constraints on rational policy development.** At the outset, the CPA had sought to adopt an integrated approach to the development of the Iraqi security sector that coordinated its myriad aspects, but this approach rapidly unraveled. A failure to view that integration as a priority and to establish the right structures to incentivize coordination among coalition personnel made it inordinately difficult to implement a unified effort toward the development and implementation of policy on Iraqi SSR.

3. **Mobilization of funding and personnel inputs from home countries.** In most nation-building operations, the mobilization of nonmilitary resources has been problematic. In Iraq, the scale of the operation and the security situation severely tested established mechanisms and the reliance on untested mechanisms via the U.S. Department of Defense delayed mobilization and deployment of resources.

4. **Balancing the long-term goals of institution-building with the short-term needs of fielding Iraqi security forces.** The coalition's

initial inclination was for sweeping reform to ensure the construction of a security sector that would underpin a transition to democracy. This, however, soon came into conflict with the increasingly pressing need to supplement coalition forces in filling the immediate security vacuum. The effort to build structures that could serve Iraq well in its transition to democracy was in constant tension with the need to respond to immediate requirements. Inevitably, some of the responses to the immediate security situation, such as a reliance on tribal guards and the creation of a more centralized police command and control structure, were contrary to the coalition's long-term political goals.

5. **Ensuring Iraqi ownership of the reform process.** For the first half of its existence, the coalition imported foreign expertise to manage Iraqi government affairs, notably in the security arena. It was only after the November 15 agreement shortened the expected timeline for the transfer of authority that the CPA focused on developing Iraqi leadership and building Iraqi capacity. Therefore, although some of the institutions and programs had been well designed, by June 2004 there was patchy Iraqi ownership as well as limited capacity in the security sector institutions. The intention was to supplement this limited capacity with international assistance, but this assistance has since fallen short of planned levels. Moreover, it remains to be seen whether the fairly extensive efforts to educate Iraqi interlocutors about best practices in SSR will have a long-term impact.

6. **Clarifying long-term security relationships.** Put simply, if the United States and its allies explicitly guarantee protection for Iraqis against external territorial aggression for the foreseeable future, then Iraq will require a small military for external defense and can concentrate on building internal security forces. If these same partners remain committed to working with Iraq on developing its security sector and Iraqi officials are committed to long-term reform, then Iraq is more likely to achieve an effective and accountable security sector. This highlights the necessity to explicitly clarify such relationships early.

The Future

Iraq's future security environment will depend on a range of factors, notably its political evolution and its economic recovery. Another important factor will be the development of its security sector into an effective but accountable part of the governance framework. As this report argues, in order to make up for past failings and to build on the successes of the past two years, the problems identified above must be addressed.

Going forward, it will be critical that Iraqi leaders and their international advisors not become preoccupied with the fielding of large numbers of security forces, which is too often used as the metric of success. Although numbers are important, it is just as vital to invest in the security sector intangibles that cannot be so easily quantified. These include the development of joint judicial and police investigatory capabilities, institutional development of national security institutions and the ministries of defense and interior, development of coordinated intelligence structures, and sustained support to the justice sector, including anticorruption programs. Iraq confronts both significant short-term needs for security forces and a long-term requirement for sustainable institutions that can serve the country in its transition to democracy. It is crucial that the first need not be met at the expense of the second.

An important need is for the Iraqi government at the highest levels to develop the capacity to make and implement security policy. Iraq's leaders lack the institutional capacity to formulate and execute policy, to systematically examine options, and to plan for the longer term. As they develop their visions for the development of the security sector, the Iraqi leadership and their international advisors will have to raise their gaze beyond implementing the current programs and start to tackle some of the basic, unanswered questions surrounding the future of the sector.

These matters are essentially political. Throughout Iraq's history, the center has used the security sector to coerce Iraq's regions and communities. In the face of the current security crisis, the tendency to go down this route is already evident, as government leaders seek to cement their own control. The reality of security in Iraq in 2005, though, is of a fragmentation of authority, as various political parties and state entities build rival security forces. The emerging Iraqi polity needs to give serious thought to the future of the security sector in terms of center-region relationships; state-society relationships; and the proportion of national resources allocated to security. Only by tackling these issues sooner rather than later can Iraq's leaders ensure that the security sector both copes with the current crisis and provides a firm foundation for a well-governed, democratic state.

Unfortunately, we need to be realistic about the likelihood of Iraqi governments having the vision to tackle these strategic issues in the short to medium term. Iraqi ministers and senior officials are likely to be more focused in coming months on their personal positions, even survival, than on long-term institution-building. The onus must therefore be on the United States, the United Kingdom, and their international partners to ensure that long-term institution-building remains on the Iraqi agenda.

Acknowledgments

This report would not have been possible without the help of numerous individuals. At RAND, Tom Sullivan provided invaluable statistical support. Nora Bensahel, David Gompert, Walter Slocombe, and Ambassador Richard Jones provided frank and insightful reviews, which greatly improved the report.

During the preparation of this report, former and serving coalition officials gave generously of their time to check facts and to provide their interpretation of decisions and events. We are particularly grateful to Fred Smith, Bruce Fein, Douglas Brand, Matt Sherman, Celeste Johnson Ward, P.J. Dermer, and Eerik Kross.

We unfortunately cannot thank everyone we spoke to, or everyone we learned from in the preparation of this study. Much of what the authors know was learned during their time with the CPA. Everything that was accomplished there, we owe to those with whom we collaborated on the effort described in this report. We therefore want to thank the coalition personnel at the CPA and at CJTF-7 who made tremendous sacrifices to do their best in a place far from home. We also want to thank courageous Iraqi officials, security force personnel, and citizens with whom we worked. They now face the task of building on everything that was done right and correcting the mistakes that were made.

Needless to say, any errors of fact and interpretation in this report are solely the responsibility of the authors.

Abbreviations

CENTCOM	Central Command
CIA	Central Intelligence Agency
CIF	Civil Intervention Force
CJTF-7	Combined Joint Task Force 7
CMATT	Coalition Military Assistance Training Team
CPA	Coalition Provisional Authority
CPATT	Civilian Police Advisory Training Team
DBE	Department of Border Enforcement
DDR	disarmament, demobilization, and reintegration
FPS	Facilities Protection Service
IAF	Iraqi Armed Forces
ICDC	Iraqi Civil Defense Corps
IGC	Iraqi Governing Council
IIG	Iraqi Interim Government
ING	Iraqi National Guard
INIS	Iraqi National Intelligence Service
IPA	international police advisor
IPS	Iraqi Police Service
IPT	international police trainer
ISF	Iraqi security forces
JCC	joint coordination center

MCNS	Ministerial Committee for National Security
MNF-I	Multinational Force–Iraq
MoD	(Iraqi) Ministry of Defense
MoI	(Iraqi) Ministry of Interior
MoJ	(Iraqi) Ministry of Justice
NIA	New Iraqi Army
NSC	National Security Council
ORHA	Office of Reconstruction and Humanitarian Affairs
OSA	Office of Security Affairs
SISG	Security Institutions Steering Group
SSR	security sector reform
TR	transition and reintegration
TRIC	Transition and Reintegration Implementation Committee

CHAPTER ONE

Introduction

Soon after the coalition occupation of Iraq began in April 2003, it became evident that prewar assumptions about the post-Saddam security situation had been unduly optimistic. The environment was not benign—in fact, it was rapidly deteriorating. Iraqi security forces had largely disintegrated, and those that remained were incapable of handling widespread criminality and political violence. The coalition confronted three security imperatives. The first task was to restore order and neutralize insurgents and terrorists. The second task was to rebuild Iraqi security forces (ISF), which could eventually take responsibility for Iraq's security. And the third task was to reconstruct and reform Iraqi security sector institutions, such as national security management institutions, the interior and defense ministries, and the justice sector, to ensure that ISF could be effective and support Iraq's political transition.

By the time that the Coalition Provisional Authority (CPA) handed authority over to the Iraqi Interim Government (IIG) on June 28, 2004, it was clear that the coalition had made little progress in the first task. Insurgent and terrorist violence was escalating, organized crime was flourishing, and the security situation was threatening both the political transition and the reconstruction program.[1] Rather than drawing down coalition forces as had been expected, the

---

[1] Rick Barton and Bathsheba Croker, *Progress or Peril? Measuring Iraq's Reconstruction*, Washington, D.C.: Center for Strategic and International Studies, September 2004.

United States and the United Kingdom had been forced to increase their troop levels.

A large part of the explanation for the state of security in June 2004 lay outside the Iraqi security sector. The aftermath of regime change was likely to be violent as the still powerful Ba'ath and Sunni elites sought to regain power and as other political groups jockeyed for position in a society awash with underemployed, armed, young men and riddled with organized crime. Efforts by coalition forces to deal with these criminal and extremist elements also fed fear and hostility in the population, which was disappointed with the expectations of rapid reconstruction.

Nonetheless, it is clear that the continuing weakness of ISF and institutions has contributed significantly to the poor security situation.[2] Without Iraqi forces able to take on security tasks, coalition forces have felt compelled to police Iraq in ways that are unpalatable to large elements of the Iraqi public.[3]

From April 2003 until the handover of power, the CPA, the Combined Joint Task Force 7 (CJTF-7), and other agencies embarked on a thoroughgoing effort to field ISF and to build security sector institutions. In assessing the progress they had made at the time the occupation came to a close, one observer argued that the coalition's lack of progress in developing the Iraqi security sector constituted an "inexcusable failure."[4]

Such assessments, however, tend to concentrate on the building of ISF capacity and on quantifiable measures of performance, such as funds disbursed, personnel trained, and equipment delivered. While these measures are an important part of the story, at least as important is the building of institutions that make up security sector

---

[2] Stephen T. Hosmer and Olga Oliker, *Countering Insurgency in Iraq: Improving Security Policies and Instruments*, Santa Monica, Calif.: RAND Corporation, forthcoming.

[3] U.S. Department of State, *Fear a Key Factor on Iraqi Political Outlook*, Opinion Analysis, Office of Research, January 18, 2005.

[4] Anthony H. Cordesman, *Inexcusable Failure: Progress in Training the Iraqi Army and Security Forces as of Mid-July 2004*, Washington, D.C.: Center for Strategic and International Studies, July 20, 2004.

capacity, as part of the government's wider ability to govern. In the long term, it will be the reconstruction and reform of these institutions that help determine the viability and nature of the new Iraqi state.

The Scope and Focus of This Report

The purpose of this report is to examine the coalition's efforts to reconstruct and reform the Iraqi security sector so as to draw lessons both for Iraq and for future reconstruction operations.

This report focuses relatively narrowly on the Iraqi security sector. It does not attempt to place security sector reconstruction in the broader context of the coalition military, political, and economic effort in Iraq. It needs to be stressed, though, that coalition decisionmakers operated within tight political, financial, and logistical constraints. They had limited freedom to make decisions, insufficient information on which to base most decisions, often had to react to circumstances,[5] and had limited ability to implement decisions once they were made.[6] Indeed, making any progress at all was incredibly difficult in the circumstances of Iraq during 2003 and 2004.

Furthermore, it is important to understand that there were few "right" answers to the questions that coalition policymakers faced. In many cases, decisionmaking was a question of balancing two or more evils rather than choosing the right course. For instance, the much criticized decisions to disband the Iraqi army and to purge Ba'athist officials from government certainly caused problems. A failure to take these decisions could, however, have led to the even worse situation of a Shiite insurgency against the coalition.

---

[5] For instance, the November 5, 2003, agreement for an early termination of CPA's mandate threw off track many of the CPA's long-term plans. In the security sector, for example, the ministerial reshuffle that accompanied the transition from the ICG to the IIG in June 2004 resulted in the removal of two ministers who had made impressive gains in grasping their portfolios.

[6] All too often, CPA decisions were not implemented because the U.S. government was unable to mobilize the required resources or to take the required decisions.

It is difficult to assess progress in security sector reconstruction and reform in any systematic manner. The approach used here is to emphasize qualitative issues over quantitative measures and to seek to identify and understand effects, positive and necessary, wherever possible. While the report does critique the coalition where appropriate, it is more valuable to understand why decisions were made and why programs were or were not implemented. This understanding can help us both to comprehend the Iraq experience and to draw lessons for the future. The Iraqi security sector is in its infancy. Future Iraqi governments and their allies will need to commit considerable intellectual and physical effort if this sector is to become an effective provider of the rule of law for a democratic Iraq. Furthermore, as the United States and its allies plan for further post-conflict reconstruction operations, they would do well to heed some of the lessons learned from Iraq.[7]

Following this introduction, Chapter Two provides background to the prewar planning that took place, primarily in the U.S. government. Specifically, the chapter describes the extent and nature of the planning that occurred and the set of assumptions under which Operation Iraqi Freedom was planned. Chapter Three provides an account of the context for security sector reform after the fall of Baghdad and of the development of each security sector element. The chapter covers coalition policymaking institutions and the evolution of coalition strategy. It then summarizes developments in the following elements of the security sector: national security institutions, the defense sector, the interior ministry, the justice sector, the intelligence services, and disarmament, demobilization and reintegration (DDR). Chapter Four provides an evaluation of the security sector under the stewardship of the coalition. The chapter first summarizes the security situation as of July 2004 and then highlights the state of each of the security sector elements by that same date. The chapter provides brief lessons learned in six key areas and concludes with observations on the way ahead.

---

[7] The United States and the United Kingdom have both established new government units to plan for post-conflict reconstruction and stabilization operations.

By concentrating on qualitative aspects of the development of the Iraqi security sector, this report deliberately does not discuss a number of important related areas that clearly affected current and future Iraqi security. First, it does not provide a comprehensive quantitative assessment of the development of ISF, in terms of either finances or numbers. These assessments are covered in depth in a range of official and unofficial reviews.[8]

Second, the report does not touch in any detail on combat operations conducted by CJTF-7 and Multinational Force–Iraq (MNF-I). Through to the end of the CPA's tenure, the coalition task force had primary responsibility for internal security in Iraq, and its performance in undertaking counterinsurgency and stability operations was far more significant for security outcomes than the performance of ISF. This remains true to a large extent at the time of this writing, but an assessment of these operations is beyond the scope of this study.

Third, this study does not address Iraq's weapons of mass destruction programs. Investigations into these programs were undertaken by the Iraq Survey Group, which did not report to the CPA. In late 2003, the CPA began to host representatives from U.S. government agencies, which sought to put in place long-term conversion and disarmament programs.

A particular strength and limitation of this report should be noted. The strength is that the report's authors held positions at the CPA during 2003 and 2004 that allowed them to participate in many of the policy decisions discussed here. They also had ready access to former CPA and military personnel and some of the CPA records in preparing this report.[9] The limitation is that this report was prepared

---

[8] Anthony Cordesman, *Strengthening Iraqi Military and Security Forces*, Washington, D.C.: Center for Strategic and International Studies, January 28, 2005. The weekly Iraq status reports issued by the Department of Defense during the life of the CPA and, since July 2004, the State Department's Iraq Policy and Operations Group (IPOG) provide regularly updated figures on ISF status.

[9] The fact that the authors were engaged in many of the policy debates discussed here may, of course, have influenced their analysis. We sought to overcome any such bias by engaging

within tight time and resource constraints. It became clear in the preparation of this report that there are many perspectives on this subject and that there is no single authoritative set of records on which to draw. Nevertheless, with this report, the activities of the CPA to reform the Iraqi security sector are now better documented than any other aspect of the CPA's activities. American and international performance in future such circumstances could be strengthened by a more comprehensive effort to document and reflect on such experience.

Assessing Success in Security Sector Reconstruction and Reform

Security sector reform (SSR) and the associated concept of security sector reconstruction are terms used more widely in the United Kingdom and donor community context than in U.S. defense circles; nonetheless, the concept describes what the coalition was seeking to achieve with Iraq's security forces and governance institutions.

SSR encompasses the transformation of the security system in a manner consistent with democratic norms and sound principles of good governance.[10] In the case of Iraq, the security sector had to be reconstructed to help provide a secure environment and reformed to support the political transition from an authoritarian state to a democratic polity.

The tenets of SSR are that first, security policy must be concerned not just with state stability but also with the well-being of the population; second, security and political and economic development are inextricably linked; and third, security problems for the population often stem from the way in which security systems operate and

---

four reviewers external to the writing team to ensure that we captured multiple perspectives on these issues.

[10] Heiner Hänggi, "Conceptualising Security Sector Reform and Reconstruction," in Alan Bryden and Heiner Hänggi, eds., *Reform and Reconstruction of the Security Sector*, Münster, Germany: Lit Verlag, 2004, pp. 3–18; Nicola Dahrendorf, ed., *A Review of Peace Operations: A Case for Change*, London: King's College London, 2003, pp. 32–39.

are organized, regulated, and resourced.[11] SSR goes beyond the uniformed services. The "security system includes the armed forces, the police and paramilitary forces, intelligence services ..., judicial and penal institutions, as well as the elected and duly appointed civil authorities responsible for control and oversight."[12]

Assessing the success of an SSR or reconstruction effort is difficult, especially since transformative changes generally take years to have an evident impact. One approach is to consider three dimensions of reform—individual, institutional, and integrative. Individual refers to changed attitudes, behaviors, and enhanced skills of individuals leading or working within a security sector. Institutional refers to the development of effective and accountable security sector institutions. Integrative refers to the degree of integration of such institutions across government and with the wider society. Progress can be measured on all three axes separately, but change is only likely to be long-lasting if reform affects all three aspects.

In this report, we have not sought to measure SSR success in any quantitative manner, but our discussions do address all three aspects of reform to enable us to make tentative, qualitative judgments.

---

[11] UK Department for International Development, *Understanding and Supporting Security Sector Reform*, London, undated; David C. Gompert, Olga Oliker, and Anga Timilsina, *Clean, Lean, and Able: A Strategy for Defense Development*, Santa Monica, Calif.: RAND Corporation, OP-101-RC, 2004.

[12] Organisation for Economic Co-operation and Development, *Security System Reform: Policy and Good Practice*, Development Assistance Committee, Network on Conflict, Peace and Development Co-operation, October 1, 2003.

CHAPTER TWO

Prewar Planning for the Iraqi Security Sector

When the U.S. government began planning for the postwar reconstruction of Iraq, the primary focus was on ensuring that humanitarian requirements were met.[1] The interagency planning structure that took shape starting in late summer and early fall 2002 included an Iraq Relief and Reconstruction Working Group.[2] This was chaired by National Security Council (NSC) staffers and incorporated representatives from a broad range of agencies. It focused primarily on issues of food and water supply, refugee flows, responses to the use of weapons of mass destruction, and other humanitarian issues. There were some efforts within both the U.S. Department of Defense (through the Office of Special Plans, the renamed Gulf Affairs subgroup of the Near East and South Asia office)[3] and the U.S. Department of State (through the "Future of Iraq" project, begun in July 2002) to think about the need to rebuild governance and security structures, but this was seen as secondary to the humanitarian effort, which received the bulk of planning attention.[4]

---

[1] This chapter draws in part on interviews conducted between October 2003 and December 2004 with representatives of ORHA, CENTCOM, OSD, the CPA, and other U.S. government agencies.

[2] Although work was initiated in July 2002, effective planning did not begin until late 2002 once the respective roles and missions of the Departments of Defense and State had been resolved.

[3] A part of the larger office of the Under Secretary of Defense for Policy.

[4] James Fallows, "Blind into Baghdad," *The Atlantic Monthly*, January/February 2004.

In January 2003, when the U.S. Defense Department was formally given the lead for postwar planning[5] and the Office of Reconstruction and Humanitarian Affairs (ORHA) was established, it was envisioned that security issues, including the rebuilding of institutions and forces, would be the responsibility of military personnel, rather than of civilians. By February, ORHA planning had changed. Each ministry, including defense, interior, and the intelligence services, would have a coalition senior advisor and ministry advisory team, which would work with what ministry staff remained after the senior Ba'athist leadership had been removed. However, the specifics of reform of these ministries were not well developed. Moreover, although the question of who would take on responsibility for coordinating and planning for security within Iraq was raised in ORHA planning efforts during February 2003, it was not answered by the time that ORHA deployed.

Shortly before the war began, the NSC started pulling together briefing materials on postwar planning. The road map for reconstruction thus developed was approved by the President on March 27, 2003, after the start of the war. This guidance called on the Defense and State Departments to develop a plan for de–Ba'athification; it also outlined guidelines for disarmament, demobilization, and reintegration of the Iraqi army and for the creation of civilian-controlled, apolitical armed forces for Iraq. The road map envisioned the use of extant Iraqi military units in reconstruction work, an approach that both Departments of Defense (Office of Special Plans) and State (Future of Iraq) planners had postulated. It called for the dismantlement of the Special Republican Guard, the Republican Guard, and paramilitary structures and for the creation of a core of a new force, consisting of three to five divisions and geared to self-defense. Internal security forces were seen as remaining under the control of the Iraqi Ministry of Interior (MoI).[6]

---

[5] By National Security Presidential Decision Directive 24.

[6] The fact that U.S. planners concentrated on the defense and interior ministries indicates that they failed to understand manner in which order was maintained in Iraq, which was primarily through a network of secret police agencies.

For all aspects of reconstruction, including security, it was expected that coalition forces and personnel would hand over control to functioning Iraqi ministries by June 2003. Right up until the point of ORHA's deployment to Baghdad in April 2003, it was thought that the predominantly non–Ba'ath Party makeup of the police force meant that these personnel would be able to maintain law and order and that coalition forces would not need to get involved in policing to any great extent. Thus, plans for the reform and reconstruction of justice and police functions were based on the expectation of functioning bureaucracies, leaving coalition personnel to perform a reform and advisory role.[7]

On the military side, a concept of operations for a DDR process for the existing Iraqi military was drawn up during April, on the assumption that the Iraqi military would still exist as a formed entity. At the same time, more detailed plans for the new Iraqi armed forces were developed. U.S. Central Command (CENTCOM) and civilian planners envisioned a new Iraqi military that would begin with a three-division corps, as laid out in the NSC guidance. This force would be built in large part from the old military, which would be vetted to eliminate Ba'ath party officials and other undesirables. It would also be much smaller than past Iraqi forces, designed to be appropriate purely for defensive missions and under civilian control. The DDR process was seen as a key mechanism. Planners believed that DDR would also facilitate the use of former military personnel for reconstruction work and potentially for security operations. Consequently, psychological operations carried out by coalition military forces during the combat phases instructed Iraqi military personnel to stay in formation as they surrendered.

---

[7] Martin Howard, then deputy chief of the United Kingdom's Defence Intelligence Staff, told the House of Commons, regarding coalition planning in April 2003: "I am not aware of anything from my knowledge where we explicitly looked at how we should deal with policing in the aftermath of conflict." UK House of Commons Defence Committee, *Evidence of Mr Martin Howard, Lt General John McColl, Major General Nick Houghton and Major General Bill Rollo*, HC 65-ii, January 6, 2005.

CHAPTER THREE

Reforming Iraq's Security Sector

This chapter examines how the Coalition Provisional Authority and other elements of the coalition undertook the reconstruction and reform of Iraq's security sector. It begins by outlining the context, detailing how the environment largely negated the assumptions on which planning had been based, and describing how policy was made and how the policy and strategy evolved. Next, it outlines developments in each of the component parts of the security sector. The areas covered are the national security institutions, the defense sector, the interior ministry, the justice sector, the intelligence services, and disarmament, demobilization, and reintegration.

The Context

The situation on the ground in Iraq during April 2003 differed fundamentally from what had been expected. During the final phases of major combat operations, it became clear that even those Iraqi military units with which the coalition had been in contact were not going to exist as formed units that could be put through a formal DDR process or used to assist with internal security. All Iraqi conscripts deserted, and the officer corps returned to their homes; Iraqi military facilities were comprehensively looted.[1] The largely conscript border

---

[1] A number of senior military officers argue that they were offered the use of formed Iraqi military units in the dying days of the war that could have been deployed under coalition

security forces also melted away, as did much of the police force. The now decapitated police force was only gradually and partially brought back to work from May onward.[2] The assumption that the coalition would be able to rely on intact Iraqi internal security forces to maintain order thus proved false from the start.

This left a "security gap" as criminal disorder swept the cities and insurgent and terrorist violence began to take root after the end of major combat operations.[3] Coalition forces could not, by structure, training, or mission, effectively fill this gap. Nor was there anyone within the ORHA structure with responsibility for this area. The looting and criminality that broke out after the fall of the regime not only caused a great deal of physical destruction but also undermined the reputation and hence legitimacy of the coalition from the outset.[4]

The relatively rapid constitution of former regime elements insurgent networks in the weeks after the invasion, combined with the outbreak of nationalist and religious resistance in Sunni areas and an influx of foreign fighters, meant that the assumption of a smooth and rapid transition to post-combat operations proved false. The escalation in insurgent and terrorist effectiveness during 2003 and early 2004, exacerbated by the confrontation with Moqtada al-Sadr's Jaish al-Mahdi, meant CJTF-7 had to conduct higher-intensity counterterror and counterinsurgency operations, despite its lack of training or resources for the mission.

The collapse of the Iraqi state and the rising levels of violence and crime meant that the prewar hopes for a rapid handover of responsibility for security and withdrawal of coalition forces were disappointed. However, the assumptions on which the post-conflict

---

command to police urban areas. However, by mid-April 2003, CENTCOM recognized that these units no longer existed.

[2] In some areas, coalition military units initially dismissed all the local police whom they perceived as ineffective, brutal, or corrupt.

[3] The presence of this "security gap" in the immediate aftermath of regime collapse had been discussed long before the fall of Baghdad. See, for example, Robert B. Oakley, Michael J. Dziedzic and Eliot M. Goldberg, eds., *Policing the New World Disorder: Peace Operations and Public Security*, Washington, D.C.: National Defense University, 1998.

[4] L. Paul Bremer III, "What I Really Said About Iraq," *New York Times*, October 8, 2004.

phase had been planned meant that CJTF-7 was not manned, equipped, trained, or postured to conduct extended counterinsurgency or stabilization operations. Likewise, neither ORHA nor the CPA had deployed with the plans, personnel, or resources needed to undertake rapid and thoroughgoing nation-building.[5] The lack of security, limited progress on reconstruction, and tactical missteps[6] led to a gradual decline in popular consent for the coalition. This in turn hampered progress on security.

The Actors Responsible for Making and Implementing Policy

There were a number of institutions involved in planning and implementing security sector reform in Iraq. The key local players were CENTCOM, CJTF-7, the CPA, and the U.S. Central Intelligence Agency (CIA). The CPA and CJTF-7 represented two parallel chains of command reaching ultimately back to the Secretary of Defense and the President of the United States.[7] CJTF-7 had the lead on security operations, but there was shared responsibility for the development of the Iraqi security sector. The CPA provided policy oversight and the vision for institutional development and reform. CJTF-7 was explicitly responsible for ISF capacity-building in relation to the Iraqi Civil Defense Corps (ICDC) but was also de facto responsible for much of the Iraqi police. During the life of the CPA, CJTF-7 formally took over the task of building the capacity of the Iraqi army (through the Coalition Military Assistance Training Team [CMATT]) and the police (through the Civilian Police Advisory Training Team [CPATT]) in the spring of 2004.

---

[5] Defined as the building of state governance capacity.

[6] These included heavy-handed military tactics when conducting search operations.

[7] A lessons learned memo prepared for the CPA administrator on May 23, 2004, by the Office of Policy Planning and Analysis argued: "There was never a single effort to achieve our goals in Iraq, but two primary efforts, led by the ... CPA and ... CJTF-7 ...." It went on to elaborate: "There were two different plans for Iraq's reconstruction: the CPA's Strategic Plan and CJTF-7's campaign plan."

Sometimes, coordination and integration of planning for the security sector were good,[8] but at other times the CPA and CJTF-7 had differing views and pursued conflicting initiatives.[9] As a result of the lack of CPA capacity during much of 2003 in terms of either policymaking or implementation, much of the early drive for particular initiatives, such as the ICDC or accelerated police recruiting, came from CJTF-7 or from CENTCOM.[10]

Within the military chain of command, many of the major initiatives were conceptualized within CENTCOM.[11] However, two important problems shaped the effectiveness of CENTCOM and CJTF-7 planning and implementation. First, since they did not control all aspects of coalition security sector policy, CENTCOM and CJTF-7 had to depend on the successful implementation of initiatives undertaken by others to meet their objectives. For instance, from the outset, military planning had assumed that an Iraqi Intelligence Service would be stood up rapidly to support Iraqi and coalition forces. When this did not happen in a timely, coordinated manner, the effectiveness of ISF and coalition operations were compromised. Likewise, a DDR program to deal with the militias, as well as with former soldiers, was an important component of military

---

[8] Indeed, compared with many other nation-building operations, the CPA and CJTF-7 did represent a major achievement in integrating civilian and military organizations and personnel.

[9] For instance, CENTCOM moved ahead with the development of an Iraqi Counter-Terrorist Force in the fall of 2003 even though CPA advisors in the MoI and the OSA had not expressed a need for such a unit within the police or army. Another long-running policy dispute was over the desire of military commanders to expand and upgrade the ICDC at the expense of the longer-term development of the IAF.

[10] The most significant initiative was probably the ISF acceleration program in late summer 2003, nicknamed "30k in 30 days," which mandated a rapid increase in the numbers of ISF, notably Iraqi police. Recruitment, training, and equipping of this number were largely the responsibility of CJTF-7 units.

[11] An important example was the concept of making the transition in a phased manner from control by coalition forces to ISF. This became a key principle behind coalition military strategy. The intention was to gradually withdraw coalition forces from Iraqi towns and provinces as ISF and Iraqi governance structures became able to maintain order and stable government.

postwar planning, but CJTF-7 was unable to persuade the CPA of the importance of this initiative.[12]

Second, the uncertainty within CJTF-7 over what sort of campaign was being conducted undermined the effectiveness of CJTF-7 operations in support of Iraqi security forces. During 2003, CJTF-7 provided ad hoc support to ISF, concentrating its main effort on operations against insurgents and terrorists. British forces in Multi-National Division (South East) formally adopted support of the Iraqi Police Service (IPS) as their key line of operations in December 2003. But it was not until the spring of 2004 that CJTF-7 revised its mission to emphasize support to the IPS as a main task and only in the summer of 2004 that the military campaign plan was revised to adopt a counterinsurgency approach.

Within CPA, policymaking and implementation were hampered by disunity and under-resourcing. As ORHA transitioned into the CPA in early May 2003, senior advisors for National Security (Walter Slocombe) and Interior (Bernard Kerik) deployed to Iraq. Their original brief had been to concentrate, respectively, on the defense and intelligence sectors and on police and law enforcement. Ambassador L. Paul Bremer, however, favored the idea of a single CPA director with oversight over the security sector as a whole and asked Slocombe to take on that role. Slocombe therefore sought not just to oversee the creation of a defense ministry but also to coordinate planning for the building of intelligence institutions and internal security functions, including police. He and his office were also assigned responsibility for Iraq's national security institutions writ large, to ensure that Iraq had a process for formulating, coordinating, and implementing its national security strategy. [13]

In practice, the complexity of these varied programs, the lack of staff, and disparate views of what the reconstruction task entailed made it all but impossible to implement a coordinated approach. By

---

[12] As discussed below, the CPA began to seriously address the militia issue only at the end of 2003.

[13] Interviews with former CPA officials. See also Walter B. Slocombe, "Iraq's Special Challenge: Security Sector Reform 'Under Fire'," in Bryden and Hänggi (2004), pp. 231–255.

early July 2003, Slocombe narrowed his remit to focus on the New Iraqi Army (NIA) and proto-MoD programs, all of which had to be built from scratch. Kerik, meanwhile, ran police operations in Baghdad, instigating an effort to recruit police personnel and get them on the streets as well as personally overseeing their operations. MoI advisory staff did not begin work on the institutional development of the ministry and the police force (nationally and regionally) until the fall of 2003. A series of other advisors ran the justice and prisons program, with varying degrees of attention to institution-building. Although all these offices reported to the CPA administrator, there was no further attempt to develop a coordinated or integrated view of the Iraqi security sector until the fall of 2003.[14]

The third local player after the coalition forces and the CPA was the CIA. As discussed below, the CIA, along with its British counterparts, had responsibility for building an Iraqi intelligence capability. However, although Slocombe's initial brief had included intelligence, neither the CPA nor CJTF-7 had effective oversight of this program until early 2004. It was not until that spring that efforts were initiated to coordinate the embryonic Iraqi National Intelligence Service (INIS) with other parts of the Iraqi security sector—which were themselves discovering a need for intelligence capacities.

All the local organizations and personnel in Iraq also reported to agencies and governments in their home countries. At times, the views of those institutions would prove to be at odds with those of the leadership in Baghdad, creating tension both for and within staffs. CPA staff, particularly, complained of efforts to "micromanage" operations from Washington, where not only the Defense Department but also the National Security Council, State Department, and other agencies often took a daily interest in events in Iraq and sought to influence them both through top-down directives and through direct communications with staff members in Iraq. Washington's involvement may have been helpful had there been a single office

---

[14] Interviews with CPA personnel, fall 2003, summer 2004; personal experience of authors.

responsible for Iraq policy that was operating to a single vision and plan. Such an office never existed.

Evolving Strategies

With funding from the first U.S. supplemental, the CPA began to implement plans for the development of the NIA and for police training in the early summer of 2003. These programs accelerated in the fall of 2003 as the ICDC was expanded and police training accelerated. Future programs for ISF were boosted by the FY 2004 supplemental request that passed through Congress in the early fall of 2003.

These programs were captured in the July 2003 version of the CPA's (first) strategic plan, which summarized programmatic timelines and milestones for the development of Iraq's security sector. However, the plan was more a compilation of existing programmatic initiatives than a prioritized set of coordinated actions.

The first attempt to take a comprehensive look at the Iraqi security sector was in the form of a Security Sector Synchronization Exercise, conducted in October 2003 by the CPA and CENTCOM. This exercise concluded that coalition plans to date had been developed in a stovepiped manner with little attention paid to dependencies and coordination between different policies and programs. The exercise outbrief noted that the accelerated force development program was not being accompanied by the rapid buildup of governance institutions, such as ministries, and that the coalition lacked concepts for the roles, missions, and long-term futures of ISF. The exercise also noted that a comprehensive DDR process was required along with greater attention to subnational command and control structures.[15]

Shortly after this exercise, the November 15 agreement forced CPA and CJTF-7 to focus on what more could be done to improve Iraqi security institutions by the end of June 2004, the date set by the agreement for the transfer of authority. In part as a response to this change, the exercise findings and the deteriorating security situa-

---

[15] CPA, *Security Sector Synchronization Exercise Outbrief*, October 11, 2003.

tion,[16] in November and December, work was undertaken on a more coordinated and strategic approach to the security sector. In November, British Representative to Iraq Sir Jeremy Greenstock proposed that additional work be undertaken on developing joint coalition-Iraqi command and control structures, notably at the provincial level.[17] In December, the CPA's policy planning office produced a paper entitled *Iraq: Integrated Security Sector Development*.[18] This paper laid "out a vision for the development of the Iraqi security sector to meet both immediate security needs and to lay the foundations for long-term stability"; its purpose was "to provide a structured framework within which crucial, and urgent, policy and operational decisions can be made by CPA, CJTF-7, CENTCOM and national capitals."[19]

Also in December, David Gompert, the incoming replacement to Slocombe, and his staff developed a concept paper on Iraqi national security institution-building.[20] This paper outlined nine elements of the Iraqi national security system that would need to be built to deal with short- and long-term requirements.[21]

Gompert's responsibilities differed from Slocombe's; he had a much more explicit mandate to take a broad oversight of the Iraqi security sector and to engage with the Iraqi leadership. This charter was prompted by the CPA's recognition after November 15 that greater coherence was required if the Iraqi security sector was to be

---

[16] November 2003 saw an upsurge in attacks on the coalition, followed in December by an escalation in CJTF-7 security operations.

[17] CPA, *Security Sector Reform: An Example of Structures Designed for Counter-Insurgency and for The Transition*, November 29, 2004.

[18] CPA, *Iraq: Integrated Security Sector Development*, Office of Policy Planning, December 4, 2003.

[19] CPA, *Iraq: Integrated Security Sector Development*, Office of Policy Planning, December 4, 2003.

[20] CPA, *Framework for Iraqi National Security Institution Building*, December 10, 2003.

[21] The elements were: coalition policy criteria; tenets of effective and democratic Iraqi national security; national security structural concepts; processes; law, authority, and regulation; general capabilities; people; infrastructure; and rough Iraq national security budget estimates.

institutionalized effectively and that the Iraqi leadership had to be rapidly engaged in the construction of national security institutions.

The Security Institutions Steering Group (SISG), discussed in more detail below, became the mechanism for coordinating policy within the coalition. Its conclusions in turn formed the basis for formal discussions with Iraqi leaders as the coalition began to transfer decisionmaking authority to the Iraqi Governing Council (IGC) and to interim ministers.

As this coordinated work on institutional development gathered pace in the spring of 2004, a number of significant milestones reshaped the program. First, in January 2004, the U.S. Defense Department dispatched a security force assessment team to Iraq. This team inquired into progress with the development of Iraq's security forces. It concluded that delays in the ISF development program, particularly the failure to bring in sufficient civilian trainers for the police, and the deteriorating security situation, made it necessary to, inter alia, transfer resources from the NIA program to the police and ICDC programs and that both the police program and the NIA program should be brought under the control of CJTF-7 to improve implementation.[22] Some of these recommendations were accepted; we discuss these below.

Second, in April 2004, the coalition stumbled into simultaneous confrontations with former regime elements and jihadist insurgents in Fallujah and Jaish al-Mahdi in South Central and Sadr City. During these confrontations, many in the ISF (ICDC, IPS, and NIA) proved unable or unwilling to fight. This led to programmatic setbacks[23] and to a refocusing of the coalition's force generation efforts on leadership and specialist training.

---

[22] Pamela Hess, "DOD, State Need Billions for Iraq," United Press International, April 21, 2004.

[23] For example, the loss of police personnel and equipment.

Elements of the Iraqi Security Sector

This section provides brief, qualitative accounts of the CPA's efforts to develop the various institutions that make up Iraq's security sector. It deals with Iraqi national security institutions, the defense sector, the interior ministry, the justice sector, infrastructure security, the intelligence services, and disarmament, demobilization, and reintegration.

National Security Institutions

Although U.S. NSC guidance for reconstruction called for an NSC structure for Iraq from the outset, it took several months for this to begin. Walter Slocombe, the first senior advisor for national security affairs to the CPA, focused his attention primarily on the Iraqi Ministry of Defense and military structures. Slocombe's office had developed a concept for a National Security Advisory Council that would engage Iraqis in a dialogue on security affairs; however, Slocombe felt that serious work in this area needed to wait for emergence of more legitimate Iraqi political institutions. In light of the November 15 agreement, his successor, David Gompert, took on the task of ensuring that Iraq had a functioning security bureaucracy after the occupation ended.

To build effective Iraqi coordinating bodies, however, there first had to be coordination among the various coalition agencies responsible for national security in Iraq. While there had been informal coordination before then, the formal mechanism for this coordination became the SISG, inaugurated on December 18, 2003. This group met every week or two weeks and involved an intensive program of papers and briefings on all national security–related issues.[24] Although the process did not resolve all the issues, it provided coordinated coalition positions in a number of critical areas that were shared with the IGC, starting early in 2004. The dialogue

---

[24] The SISG brought together the CPA's Offices of National Security Affairs and Policy Planning; advisors to the Iraqi ministries of Justice, Interior, and Foreign Affairs; the British representative to the CPA; CJTF-7 staff branches; and coalition intelligence agencies.

with the IGC's security committee and notably its chair, Dr. Iyad Allawi, laid the basis for the emergence of more formal joint Iraqi-coalition national security institutions. It also provided the opportunity for coalition personnel to discuss their vision for a "developed" security sector in Iraq with the IGC security committee.

The March 2004 transitional administrative law[25] delineated some crucial aspects of national security decisionmaking. For instance, it laid down the requirement for a Presidency Council request and National Assembly approval of any dispatch abroad of the armed forces and the National Assembly's role in treaty ratification. It also made clear the role of the Presidency Council as ceremonial commander in chief of the armed forces, with operational command authority flowing from the prime minister to the minister of defense to the military chain of command of the Iraqi Armed Forces (IAF). However, while this defined the overall framework, as the Iraqi staffs of the various ministries took more control in preparation for the handover of power at the end of June, the need for coordination at the ministry level became increasingly clear.

The national security structure eventually implemented was one designed by the CPA senior advisor for national security and his staff, in consultation with the IGC National Security Committee. It envisioned regular meetings of the "power" ministers (Defense, Justice, Foreign Affairs, Interior, and Finance, with others invited to specific meetings as necessary) in a structure dubbed the Ministerial Committee for National Security (MCNS). The senior military advisor to the government of Iraq and the director general of the Iraqi Intelligence Service would also participate in these meetings, which would be chaired by the head of government (Ambassador Bremer prior to handover of power, the prime minister thereafter). In addition, the post and office of national security advisor were created to coordinate among the ministries in preparation for MCNS meetings and to ensure national security coordination more broadly. This advisor was

---

[25] The transitional administrative law, issued in March 2004, was in effect the interim constitution that would govern Iraq until an elected constitutional assembly could write a new constitution.

also to provide impartial advice to the head of government and the ministers.

The MCNS was convened for the first time in March 2004 and met a number of times before it was officially created by CPA Order 68 on April 4, 2004. The order provided for the participation, by invitation, of the commander of MNF-I, at that time Lieutenant General Ricardo Sanchez. Mowaffaq al-Rubaie, an IGC member, was named interim national security advisor on April 9. Iyad Allawi, as chair of the IGC Security Committee, also sat in on meetings starting in April.[26] The MCNS met frequently from early April onward as the body faced the simultaneous crises in South Central, Sadr City, and Fallujah.

The creation of this structure at a time of crisis meant that the MCNS had an impact almost immediately, although this was more on the style of decisionmaking than in respect of major strategic decisions. Putting the interim ministers in regular contact with each other and with Ambassador Bremer and General Sanchez empowered the ministers to convey their views as key decisions were made regarding the way ahead in combat and negotiations with insurgents. The ministers began to take on the roles of decisionmakers in Iraq's government, interacting with each other and their head of state. The forum also enabled the interim ministers to raise other issues with interministerial implications and to communicate their needs to CPA and CJTF-7 leadership in a more intimate forum than that allowed for by working through the IGC or through bilateral interaction with senior advisors. This process helped cement the MCNS as a true governmental structure months before transfer of authority.

In addition to dealing with day-to-day crisis management, the MCNS and its deputies committee, supported by ministry staff assigned to the office of the national security advisor, also worked to develop a more structured and proactive, Iraqi-led response to the threat of jihadist terrorism. This involved first developing a coordi-

---

[26] Allawi's participation raised questions about the propriety of having a member of a quasi-legislative body—the IGC—involved in an executive branch structure, but this was deemed necessary given the precarious security situation.

nated counterterrorism strategy, including an action plan delineating the responsibilities of various ministries and security agencies.[27] Although it had limited practical impact, this strategy did improve interministerial coordination, notably by engaging more effectively with the religious *awqaf*.[28] Second, the MCNS oversaw working-level activity by Iraqi ministries and the coalition to coordinate security for the upcoming Shi'ite festival of Arbaeen, which involved the transit of large numbers of pilgrims to religious sites. The pilgrims were likely targets of terrorist attacks as had been demonstrated by March 2004 attacks during the holiday of Ashura.

When the IIG emerged from tripartite negotiations among the CPA, the United Nations, and the IGC in June 2004, the new government continued to make use of the MCNS but reshaped it according to Iraqi needs. Known to Iraqis as the Supreme or Higher Security Committee, the committee essentially formed an inner circle of key "power" ministers around Prime Minister Allawi. The committee dealt with immediate security issues but also supervised work on a national security strategy that was drafted with coalition assistance in the summer of 2004.[29]

National Security Institutions: Lessons and Implications. Even though the CPA started late in its efforts to build national security decisionmaking institutions for Iraq, the MCNS started off well in this area. Its continuation by the IIG demonstrated the appropriateness of the model, notably for improving coordination between Iraqi ministers and the coalition. However, even under the CPA, limited progress was made on institutionalizing lower-level coordinating structures.

---

[27] Andrew Rathmell, "Building Counterterrorism Strategies and Institutions: The Iraqi Experience," presented at Three Years After: Next Steps in the War on Terror, RAND conference, Washington, D.C., September 8, 2004.

[28] The Iraqi religious establishment was split into three *awqaf*: Sunni, Shia, and Christian.

[29] The draft strategy was never endorsed by the prime minister. Elements of the strategy, however, emerged in January 2005 in a public strategy paper issued by Prime Minister Allawi shortly before that month's elections.

Operational/Tactical Command, Control, and Coordination

As ISF began to play an increasingly important role in internal security, the CPA had to ensure that they had adequate arrangements for command and control and co-ordination with coalition forces. On the military side, this proved relatively easy to achieve, since the ICDC was under the control of coalition forces and army units were likewise handed off to coalition forces once they had graduated from training. Building an Iraqi joint headquarters that would play an expanding role in command-ing the IAF after the transfer of authority was an important part of the long-term IAF development program.

The IPS posed a more difficult challenge because it was not under the control of coalition forces. Throughout the life of the CPA, the MoI and IPS lacked a clear vision for its nationwide structure as well as the capacity to control and communicate with subordinate units, with other ISF, and with coalition forces.[30] As an interim stopgap, CJTF-7 developed joint coordination centers (JCCs) at provincial and municipal levels. These communications hubs, manned by coalition forces and ISF, provided a coordi-nation and communications backbone that linked coalition forces with the IPS and other ISF. During the spring and summer of 2004, these JCCs began to provide much-needed coordination; they also deconflicted situations in which two or more forces were engaged.[31] The long-term vision was that these JCCs would transition into police operations centers, since police primacy was viewed as the key to successful internal security operations.

The continued success of the committee and its successor struc-tures will depend on the recognition by the ministries and the office of the prime minister of the need for effective coordination of policy and for effective coordinating institutions. The Iraqi government needs to assign appropriate priority to this structure, ensure that its role in decisionmaking remains central, and have a capable and trusted national security advisor with the capacity to work with min-isters, to advise the prime minister, and to run a staff that ensures smooth coordination of policy. This is a challenge in modern democ-racies, and it will be difficult in Iraq. If this is not achieved, there will

---

[30] In April 2004, the lack of a national police operations center became of vital concern, but neither the CPA nor CJTF-7 were able to provide the necessary communications infra-structure in a timely manner. It was only in June/July 2004 that priority was given to out-fitting a national operations center that would allow the IIG to have access to real-time infor-mation on events across Iraq.

[31] Indeed, one of the motives for the JCC concept was to reduce the number of incidents in which coalition forces fired upon the IPS.

be a risk of factionalization of the various ministries as they build their own fiefdoms. While the international community can do little to influence the nature and direction of such factionalization, it can help develop the institutional capacity at the center of government that will demonstrate the value of a professional and expert decision-making apparatus to future Iraqi governments.

The Defense Sector

The Iraqi defense sector consisted of the Ministry of Defense[32] and the Iraqi Armed Forces. The sector came to include the Iraqi Civil Defense Corps, which was subordinated to the MoD at the time of the ministry's creation in March 2004.

The Defense Ministry. The coalition had expected to reform the defense ministry through de-Ba'athification and emplacement of an advisory team, as with other ministries. However, with the disintegration of the Iraqi army, the CPA decided to formally abolish the ministry, which in any case did not provide an acceptable basis on which to build a modern, professional, democratically accountable and civilian-led defense sector.[33] The MoD, along with the army, therefore had to be rebuilt from the ground up. The Office of Security Affairs (OSA)[34] was tasked with this effort. OSA served both as the CPA's defense policy office and as the de facto MoD until the new MoD was established on March 21, 2004.[35] To support the New Iraqi Army in the absence of an MoD, OSA created a subordinate office called the Defense Support Agency (DSA).[36] In addition, CMATT, responsible for creating the NIA, initially was under OSA.

---

[32] The CPA settled on a British spelling of "defence" in the title of the new MoD. However, for the sake of consistency, in this report we use the U.S. spelling "defense" throughout.

[33] CPA Order 2, Dissolution of Entities with Annex A, May 23, 2003.

[34] Later, the Office of the Senior Advisor for National Security Affairs (ONSA).

[35] CPA Order 61, Amendment to Order 45, February 22, 2004.

[36] The plan was for DSA to first take on the support functions, such as logistics and personnel, before moving onto policy issues. One senior CPA official who was intimately involved in the Iraqi defense sector development characterized DSA as "an MoD without a brain."

CPA advisors initially felt that the creation of the MoD should await the creation of units for them to oversee and of Iraqi political authorities to provide oversight. The CPA believed that the security ministries would likely be the last to "graduate" to full Iraqi control. Officials hoped to wait until Iraqi political structures and parties were mature enough for the CPA to discern which actors could be trusted with the responsibility for developing a defense sector that would not oppress the Iraqi people.

The November 15 agreement forced an acceleration of the process. Formal planning to establish an MoD was at that point still in its infancy, but it immediately got into high gear. Fred Smith, a U.S. Defense Department senior executive, was asked to lead this effort. After the agreement, OSA also took on the task of creating wider national security institutions by coordinating policy development across the CPA, with CJTF-7 and the CIA as well as with the IGC and its Security Committee.[37]

OSA was a small office, and its staff comprised American, British, Australian, Czech, and Estonian civilian and military defense specialists, along with a Spanish contingent (until withdrawn after the Spanish elections in the spring of 2004), an Italian contingent, and occasional assistance from other personnel. Thus, a staff with significant experience and insight into the strengths and weaknesses of several defense systems collaborated in the creation of the new MoD. (See Figure 3.1 for an overview of the final organization.) Aside from creating the normal functions of a defense ministry from scratch, the team also had to recruit and train MoD personnel and provide political leadership. Recruitment got the first priority; contracting, second; and budgeting, third. Policy development did not receive a high priority, since it was felt that, with the likely presence of the United States and coalition countries in Iraq for the foreseeable future, this capability would develop over time, whereas building the institutional machinery necessary to budget, man, and equip the army was an immediate need.

---

[37] The office's mandate shrunk in March 2004 when CMATT was placed under the command of the CJTF-7 with DSA in direct support.

Figure 3.1
Iraqi Ministry of Defense Organization

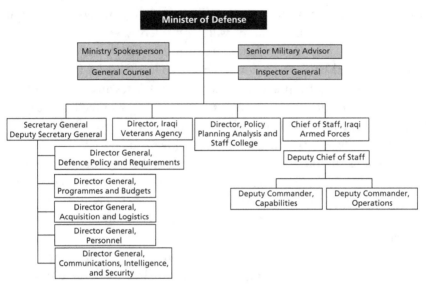

SOURCE: CPA, Office of National Security Affairs.
RAND *MG365-3.1*

CPA staff carried out their design work with limited Iraqi input. Although some trusted Iraqi personnel were involved in specific decisions, relating particularly to personnel, the only Iraqis systematically engaged in this policy area were those on the Security Committee of the Iraqi Governing Council, who began receiving briefings on the MoD and other security structures in early 2004. As a result, the MoD was designed, staffed, and created with very little input from Iraqis on a day-to-day level, except when CPA staff explicitly sought the views of former military personnel and academics—a sporadic effort, hampered by limited information, security constraints, and staff shortages

Recruitment for the MoD proved challenging. CPA staff undertook a yearlong outreach program that involved interviews of leading candidates from all segments of Iraqi society throughout the country.

This effort included academic outreach, contacts through Iraqis working with the CPA, word of mouth, and significant assistance from party and community leaders. The effort had mixed success, but in the end, thousands of names were compiled, several hundred people interviewed, and a small core hired to perform jobs at the director-general level and below. Despite the difficulties the CPA had in understanding Iraqi social structures and assessing the diligence and trustworthiness of candidates, this effort produced a cadre of largely capable, trustworthy mid- to senior-level leaders who risked their lives daily to work in the new Iraqi government.

Because the old defense ministry was staffed exclusively by uniformed officers, with virtually no civilians, most of those hired to lead the new MoD either were former officers or were civilians with no experience in security matters. As a result, training became a major concern.

There were two components of training. The first components involved traveling to Washington, D.C., for three weeks of training: a two-week course at the Near East South Asia Center at the National Defense University followed by a one-week course at the U.S. Institute of Peace. This effort, begun in the spring of 2004, was thought to provide the future leadership of Iraq's MoD with a foundation of understanding of civilian control of the military, some basics in defense sector management and issues, and (not unimportantly) a look at a successful, functional democratic country. The second component comprised short classes and on-the-job training in Iraq, supervised by defense advisors from coalition countries. They were assisted briefly by contract trainers who provided courses on the various components of a defense ministry, ranging from policy to logistics.

Given the very limited time available to stand up the MoD and the need for staff to be available and working, some questioned the value of training abroad. However, CPA advisors in Iraq were short staffed and spread thin, so their capacity to provide consistent training in the early stages was limited. There were also significant benefits to removing Iraqi officials from the pressures of day-to-day life in Baghdad.

MoD: Lessons and Implications. While the general design of the MoD was sound, despite limited Iraqi input, the recruitment and staffing effort was significantly hampered by the time constraint created by the agreement to turn full authority over to the Iraqis by July 2004. To have some institutional structures in place prior to handover, advisors believed that an MoD had to be stood up by April 1, 2004. This meant that there was less than five months to create an MoD from scratch. The limited time also exacerbated the difficulty of the effort to identify appropriate and competent personnel. The lack of Iraqi involvement in the process contributed to future problems. While there were bureaucratic and security challenges inherent in a greater Iraqi role,[38] many of those involved now feel that more effort should have been made in this sphere.

The CPA also confronted a significant trade-off between the desire to focus on young people, with limited experience in Saddam's initiative-stifling bureaucratic structures, and the need to identify competent and knowledgeable staff members, who could in turn recruit, evaluate, and train other staff. Younger staff had less familiarity with their subject areas, and older personnel invariably proved slow to accept new approaches. If the MoD development process could have been extended, it might have been possible to establish the institutions and structures that would have helped guide new staff. Despite these problems, all former CPA advisors interviewed for this report felt that the final MoD civil service leadership was in fact of high quality.

Public communication was also lacking. Since the Saddam-era armed forces had been regarded with suspicion by many of Iraq's communities, notably the Kurds, a structured, aggressive public information campaign would have been helpful in making the public, and even political leaders, aware of what the new army was and was not. Even as late as May 2004, many Iraqi leaders did not know that the army was to be significantly smaller than Saddam's army and that its mission was to be purely defensive. Educating the public on this

---

[38] Simply gaining access to the Green Zone and the Republican Palace was very difficult for Iraqi nationals.

should have been an important mission for the CPA and the new MoD. Nonetheless, it was striking to note that polls of Iraqi public opinion demonstrated quite widespread support for the new IAF.[39]

The short time frame for creating the MoD and the lack of Iraqi involvement made the fledgling ministry vulnerable to political change. The MoD was two months old in June 2004 when the new Iraqi government was installed (which promptly replaced the defense minister). A more established ministry structure, with more time for staff to learn their roles and to build and prove their capacity, would have responded better to this change. As it was, the Iraqi government inherited from the CPA a defense ministry it did not build and staffed with personnel it did not choose. This led to tensions between the CPA-appointed officials and appointees of the new minister, encouraging a number of officials to leave and undercutting the CPA's efforts to build a professional, politically neutral civil service cadre in the ministry. This was perhaps an unrealistic goal in the context of Iraq, but if there had been more time, further progress could have been made to institutionalize critical processes and to grow a cadre of capable, professional staff.[40]

The Armed Forces. Like the MoD, the IAF had to be built from scratch. Unlike the MoD, this had been the intent all along, although planners had expected to rely somewhat more on the infrastructure of the old Iraqi military than was possible following its disintegration in April 2003. The decision to formally abolish the old armed forces meant not only was there no DDR process and no Iraqi military personnel to help with security, stabilization, and reconstruction, it also meant that the CPA faced continuing problems of demands for payment by the former military personnel.[41] Some also argued that

---

[39] See, for instance, U.S. Department of State, *Opinion Analysis*, M-71-04, June 17, 2004.

[40] The presence of effective coalition advisors in the MoD after July 2004 went some way toward ensuring continuity in terms of personnel and institutional development.

[41] A stipend and pension system was created in June 2003 but was not seen as sufficient by many Iraqi officers. The CPA set the stipend to be below prior base pay but sufficient for a middle-class standard of living.

the dissolution of the military was a slap in the face to Iraqis, for whom the army was a symbol of their nation.

That said, it should be reiterated that creating a new Iraqi military was the coalition's intention from the start. Moreover, the elimination of a top-heavy, inefficient, bureaucratic structure that was reflective of the former regime was the only possible way to create an effective and efficient Iraqi military.[42] Although a DDR process might have been a more effective mechanism to determine which personnel had a role in the new force and which did not, the fact was that the old military, with its 10,000 generals, was not in keeping with the goals of a new Iraq.

Coalition planners intended to create first a three-division corps, with about 12,000 men per division. This corps could grow as needed, but the goal was to create a force that was strictly for defense and would not threaten Iraq's neighbors. There was some debate between military and civilian officials regarding whether to begin by recruiting an officer corps and then filling in all three divisions at once or by building up the force one unit at a time. A decision was made to start small and identify senior leadership later, when advisors would have more information and there would be less risk inherent in selecting senior military personnel. Coalition officials agreed that it was crucial that the new corps reflect Iraq's ethnic, regional, and religious makeup, a reversal of the Saddam-era armed forces, which had a predominantly Sunni officer corps but a predominantly Shi'ite soldiery.

Planners briefed their concept, developed with the recent experience of building the Afghan National Army in mind, to the U.S. Defense Department in early June 2003. The force they described would have limited ability to project or sustain power away from its bases and would depend on other ministries for support functions, such as health care. Per the plan, CMATT was created. Major General Paul Eaton was named to lead it. CMATT would recruit and train the military, as CPA staff did for the MoD. CMATT eventually

---

[42] Gompert, Oliker, and Timilsina (2004).

grew to about 200 personnel representing a broad range of coalition countries. Vinnell Corporation won a $48 million, one-year contract to assist with training and other support. It in turn subcontracted to MPRI for training and to SAIC for recruitment.[43]

SAIC set up recruiting stations in July, with a poster campaign to inform young people of the opportunities available in the new force. In Kurdish areas, local officials identified personnel from among the forces of Kurdish militias, and transition offices were set up to help *peshmerga* enter the armed forces. By early August, CMATT was training 1,000 new recruits. The NIA was officially created on August 7, 2003, by CPA Order 22.

Planning for the IAF would adjust throughout the occupation, even as the name of the force changed from the New Iraqi Army to Iraqi Armed Forces. In September 2003, the CPA revised its time-table for building the force, with the goal of forming 27 battalions within 12 months.[44] Additional force structures were added, including an air component, a coastal defense component, and an Iraqi counterterrorism force. Meanwhile, the passage of the $18.4 billion FY 2004 U.S. supplemental provided the necessary financial resources.

The lack of information about Iraqi society available to CPA and CMATT personnel was a continuing problem. Early on, coalition advisors assumed that only officers below the rank of colonel from the old Iraqi army would be eligible for service in the new army, believing that high-level Ba'ath party membership had been a requirement for higher military rank. When Iraqis came forward with the records of the old army, coalition staff learned that this was not the case and revised their recruiting guidelines. Later still, they learned that the database of former Iraqi military personnel on which

---

[43] Nathan Hodge, "Pentagon Agency May Train Iraqi War-Crimes Prosecutors," *Jane's Defence Weekly,* September 15, 2003; Nathan Hodge "Northrop Grumman to Train New Iraqi Army," *Jane's Defence Weekly,* July 7, 2003; Mark Fineman, "Arms Plan For Iraqi Forces Is Questioned," *Los Angeles Times,* August 8, 2003.

[44] Thom Shanker, "US Is Speeding Up Plans for Creating a New Iraqi Army," *New York Times,* September 18, 2003.

they had been basing so many of their decisions was less reliable than they might have hoped, particularly on issues regarding Ba'ath Party membership and past criminal records.[45] The need to rely on unsubstantiated and uncorroborated word-of-mouth reports—exacerbated by the limited availability of additional records (e.g., retirement documents)—to recruit and evaluate prospective soldiers, officers, and MoD personnel remained a significant problem throughout the occupation.

Desertion rates were another major problem. Iraq's first battalion of recruits, which graduated on October 4, 2003, had a particularly high rate of desertion. This was attributed to low salaries, particularly in comparison with the police and the ICDC. Pay rates were raised and hazardous duty allowances added,[46] but some CPA officials

---

[45] This database was used to vet personnel and has a somewhat interesting history. In the spring of 2003, CPA staff were approached by former Iraqi Ministry of Defense staff who reported that they had in their possession several hard drives full of personnel records of the old Ministry. These personnel were hired by CPA to create a new database for the CPA on the basis of this one, amending it so as to make it searchable for such information as Ba'ath party membership, criminal records, and so forth. Once the stipend program was begun, the database was further updated on the basis of the registration forms provided by stipend recipients. This made it possible to validate and update the information in the original database, as well as to acquire better information where there were significant gaps, such as in the records for noncommissioned officers. Iraqi personnel developed the database, entered information into it, and ran searches for the CPA's staff, all with minimal supervision. In the spring of 2004, CPA staff learned that the personnel responsible for creating the database had written the software such that certain information, specifically Ba'ath Party membership and criminal records, was "firewalled" and only readily accessible to the original coders. Thus, a search carried out by somebody else would not, for example, reveal Ba'ath Party membership. In fact, searches were at times carried out by different people and, as a result, some information provided to CPA and CJTF-7 staff reflected the full record, while others did not. When questioned, the Iraqi personnel reported that this firewalling, or password protection, was time delimited for when the responsible personnel were not available, but there is no easy way to confirm this. CPA staff interviewed for this study who doubted the time delimitation speculated that a concern that individuals not be denied pensions may have driven this situation, although some also voiced concerns about possible infiltration, and reported that there had been accusations by other Iraqi personnel to that effect. Regardless, the end result was clearly problematic. It is not clear whether the original MoD database was retained. (Interviews with CPA officials, December 2004 and January 2005.)

[46] Because the ICDC and, to some extent, the IPS were initially paid at the discretion of individual MSCs of CJTF-7, pay initially varied to a great degree across the country.

felt that the real problem was the lack of a clear mission for these forces.

What was the mission? While CENTCOM planners had from the start expected to use Iraqi military personnel for internal security, the force being built was designed with an external defense role in mind. Some coalition officials argued that the fight against external aggression was a worst-case scenario, which subsumed others and ensured that soldiers trained for it would be prepared for anything. Other officials argued that counterterror and counterinsurgency required specific training and capabilities. Moreover, internal use of the Iraqi military was politically sensitive, and many IGC members and government officials were wary of an internal role.

Operationally, the mission question was brought to a head in April 2004, when Iraq's newly trained armed forces were called upon to fight, as operations against insurgents escalated in Fallujah. An effort to deploy the Iraqi Army Second Battalion backfired when the battalion came under fire in Baghdad, on its way to Fallujah. These forces refused to continue and also rejected the option to be flown by helicopter to the battle. Coalition military advisors attributed this "mini-mutiny" to a combination of reluctance among Iraqi soldiers to fight their countrymen and a lack of effective preparation for the testing environment of urban combat.

In due course, language governing the role and mission of the armed forces was hammered out within the CPA and with the IGC, as reflected in the transitional administrative law. By the spring of 2004, it was agreed that the army's primary mission would be external defense but that in exceptional circumstances, such as the ongoing insurgency, it could be deployed internally in support of the civil authorities. From this period onward, the army training and force structure was revised to more explicitly focus on internal security and counterinsurgency operations.

The effort to create a representative force that reflected the ethnic, religious, and sectarian makeup of the country as a whole was another priority of the CPA and CJTF-7. While recruiters ensured that every unit had a mix of ethnic groups, the effort to integrate those personnel effectively was at the discretion of trainers, and some paid more attention to this than others. Officers who underwent training in Jordan reported significant tension between Arab and Kurdish recruits, to the point that the Kurds returned home unsure that they could fight in the new military.[47]

Meanwhile, the actual building of the force continued apace, with decreasing attrition over time. The March 2004 shift of CMATT to CJTF-7 control changed little in the planning for the IAF, although it did create some confusion regarding policy direction and chain of command. The Iraqi forces were, after all, to be under civilian control exercised through the MoD. That ministry was being stood up by the CPA, but the CPA no longer had a direct relationship with CMATT.

As the CPA's tenure drew to a close, the need to name senior military personnel, earlier postponed, became pressing. There was still painfully little information about the past activities of candidates, and little capacity to judge competence. Senior appointments were vetted through the IGC Security Committee, which eliminated several contenders, but the selection process remained largely unchanged. In mid-April 2004, a number of senior appointments were announced, including Chief of the General Staff General Amer Bakr al-Hashimi, who had remained politically independent throughout a military career under Saddam. The Kurdish General Babaker Zebari was named senior military advisor to the defense minister and to the government at the same time. By the time of the transfer of authority, all key positions had been filled.

In addition to the IAF proper, another military force was developed in occupied Iraq: the Iraqi Civil Defense Corps. The ICDC was born of the need of coalition commanders to have Iraqi personnel carry out certain functions. These included static defense, interpreters, and human intelligence collection, but it also involved a recognition of the need for an Iraqi face on operations—in particular, the need to have Iraqis join coalition soldiers on patrol. A combination of the initiative of individual commanders, who brought Iraqis on board

---

[47] Some reported having been threatened by their Arab colleagues and that Saddam-era symbols and ceremonies persisted in the new military.

to carry out these functions, and CENTCOM recognition of this requirement, as well as the desire to employ former military personnel and members of anti-Saddam militias as quickly as possible, all brought the ICDC formally into being.[48] Although the CPA national security leadership had been wary of the establishment of an Iraqi army too quickly, it was more accepting of the ICDC, as long as it was clear that this was a different structure from the IAF and not an alternative to it. The ICDC had minimal training and was fundamentally a support force for coalition forces, with very limited capacity for independent action.

The ICDC quickly expanded from the initial concept of squad- or platoon-size units with minimal equipment (a uniform and a weapon). While these units remained locally based and needed less support than the IAF, their mission and structures grew until they became company-size units, providing a range of functions in support of coalition forces. They were linguists, intelligence collectors, fixed-site security personnel, drivers, and disaster relief and humanitarian assistance providers. They went on patrols; participated in convoys, cordons, and checkpoints; and provided security for coalition personnel. They were also increasingly valuable as the Iraqi component of coalition military actions. They also received more equipment over time, until, with helmets, body armor, heavier weapons, and vehicles, they looked increasingly like motorized infantry.

The ICDC grew from a planned force of one battalion for each coalition division to one of 18 battalions—one per governorate. By the CPA's end, this number had, in turn, been doubled. Plans for the total force strength rose concomitantly. By the middle of February 2004, however, there were already 25,000 hired and another 3,600 being trained. When the Iraqi Interim Government took power in June 2004, plans were under way to field 40,000 ICDC personnel, a large force size in comparison to the IAF.

These numbers included a "36th Battalion" of the ICDC, made up of personnel representing five anti-Saddam militias. Created as a

---

[48] The initial plan for the ICDC was presented to CPA and Pentagon officials in the summer of 2003.

result of coalition negotiations with the political parties who had sponsored those militias, the 36th Battalion was thought to be more experienced, better trained, and more capable of independent action.

The ICDC was created to support coalition forces. It was an odd hybrid with an uncertain future. As a lightly trained support force, its mission and institutional home in an independent Iraq was unclear. Throughout the occupation, CPA, U.S. Defense Department, CENTCOM, IGC, and other coalition government officials debated the future of the ICDC. Some argued that it should be transformed into a "third force" or gendarmerie. Others felt that a national guard structure, under local government control, was the best option (Kurdish groups particularly favored this approach). Some felt that the ICDC should form the core of a reserve structure for the IAF.

The other question was which ministry would control the ICDC. On the one hand, the ICDC's mission was clearly domestic in nature. On the other hand, it was not clear that this would always be the case. Furthermore, an additional large armed force under the Ministry of Interior would give that ministry disproportionate power. Eventually, it was decided that the ICDC would be under the Ministry of Defense. As to its final status, although CPA officials had agreed that transition into a reserve would be the best option, the U.S. Secretary of Defense decided in March 2004 that the decision would be left to the IIG.

Shortly after taking power, the IIG renamed the ICDC the Iraqi National Guard (ING)[49] and made it clear that the force would come under the MoD.[50] In practice, though, the ING continued to operate in support of coalition forces. In this way, the ICDC came to form the bulk of Iraq's contribution to the military coalition.

---

[49] Albeit without the local government control, which is part of the National Guard model in the United States.

[50] The MoD strategy published in draft form by Defense Minister Hazim al–Sha'alan in December 2004 made clear that the ING was part of the MoD but tasked to operate in support of the IPS on internal security duties. Iraqi Ministry of Defense, *2005 Defense Plan,* draft, December 1, 2004.

Because the ICDC's mission was domestic from the start, it was in action throughout its existence. In some areas, ICDC units were highly respected by the public; in others, they were not. Quality and training varied greatly. There can be no doubt that having Iraqi forces capable of conducting searches and interfacing with the public was a tremendous help to the coalition. However, when called on to fight, some units proved more effective than others. During the upsurge in violence in April 2004, some ICDC personnel fought bravely, whereas others deserted or disappeared. This variance in performance should not have been surprising. In the words of one senior general in MNF-I, the coalition was naive to have expected largely untrained and poorly equipped units to perform well, or at all, in the toughest of all combat situations—urban warfare. Designed to support coalition forces, it is not surprising that the locally recruited and based ICDC members often crumbled in the face of severe intimidation and rival calls on their loyalties.

Furthermore, the use of the 36th Battalion in Fallujah led several of the Arab militias to withdraw their personnel and other Arab militiamen to refuse to fight, leaving the unit predominantly manned by Kurds. This, in turn, led to public complaints that the coalition had sent Kurds to fight the Arabs of Fallujah.

IAF: Lessons and Implications. The building of the IAF was a mixed success, a combination of well-thought-out plans and responses to immediate need, good decisions, and questionable ones. The IAF itself suffered most, perhaps, from the unclear nature of its mission. Although counterinsurgency training was added to the overall program late in the CPA's tenure, a better option might have been to leave that force as Iraq's defense against external aggression. The IAF was neither sufficiently competent nor sufficiently large to make a real contribution to the fight within Iraq, and efforts to use it in this way are not only problematic in terms of their immediate effect, but they also create real concerns for the capacity to build appropriate civil-military relations in the new Iraq. In the long term, the effort to ensure cohesion within an ethnically mixed military may also backfire, even though the goal of creating armed forces that reflect Iraqi society is to be lauded. That said, the deliberate and plans-based approach to building the IAF has led to real successes and, if continued, may result in a relatively professional military in which Iraqis can take pride.

The ICDC, now the ING, is also a mixed success. It was built quickly, haphazardly, and in response to immediate requirements. As a stopgap support force, coalition commanders believe it has proved effective in limited functions. However, some CPA officials have argued that the resources would have been better used in a more systematic program of support for the police.

The growth of the ICDC did at various times lead to calls for it to become a professional third force, in addition to the military and the police. This would have been a mistake, though, because the ING remains postured only to assist other better-trained and -equipped units. It should also be remembered that its personnel are soldiers, not policemen. At present, the ING supports the Iraqi police when the latter face levels of violence they are not equipped to handle. In the future, it is possible to envision the ING acting in support of the IAF when those forces confront an external threat of which their size precludes them handling on their own.

The failure of the ICDC and the IAF to perform consistently well when called upon to fight insurgents alongside coalition forces is a complex issue. In the case of the IAF, the argument can be made that forces created and trained to fight an external enemy should never have been asked to carry out a domestic role. Although a domestic role was always part of CENTCOM's vision, until early 2004 the CPA and the majority of its interlocutors on the IGC sought to focus the force on external defense. CMATT continued through to the spring of 2004 to focus on training recruits for external defense.

Desertions from the ICDC, meanwhile, can be attributed to a combination of their limited training and equipment and the fact that many ICDC personnel were either intimidated by or sympathetic to insurgents. A fundamental weakness underlying the ICDC concept was the lack of strong indigenous leadership; ICDC commanders were often unsure of the extent of coalition commitment to their future and reluctant to serve the "occupiers" in the face of intense local hostility.[51] More recent engagements have shown the ING to be more reliable when used in support of and led by more professional forces.

The Interior Ministry

Institution-building at the interior ministry covered both the ministry and its subordinate forces, primarily police and border enforcement.

The Ministry of Interior. Unlike the defense ministry and intelligence agencies, the MoI was not dissolved, because the coalition's intention was to hand over responsibility for policing and internal security to Iraqi institutions as soon as feasible. The CPA restructured the ministry significantly, but because much of the CPA's focus was on the physical reconstruction of the ministry and the development of its deployed forces, limited overall progress was made in developing the MoI as an institution.

The Saddam-era interior ministry had a broad range of security and administrative functions.[52] Most of these administrative functions were retained in the new MoI, but the responsibility for prisons was removed and handed to the Ministry of Justice. Conversely, the previous dual MoI-MoD control over border security was resolved with the creation of a Department of Border Enforcement within the MoI.[53]

The new ministry structure, developed jointly by CPA advisors and then interim minister Nouri Badran, was approved in November 2003 (see Figure 3.2).[54] The philosophy adopted was one of national

---

[51] The arrest of the ING commander in Diyala in September 2004 for passing information to the insurgents indicates the extent of divided loyalties among even senior ISF personnel.

[52] For example, registration of aliens and citizenship.

[53] This also included some border control and revenue collection functions that had been the preserve of the Ministry of Finance.

[54] The mission statement adopted at the time read: "The new Iraqi Ministry of Interior is a vital component in the new, democratic Iraq. The Ministry's mission is to ensure the security and safety of Iraqi citizens and of their property. It will serve Iraqi citizens of all backgrounds and beliefs. The Ministry has a central role to play in protecting the constitutional process to

Figure 3.2
Iraqi Ministry of Interior Approved Organization, November 2003

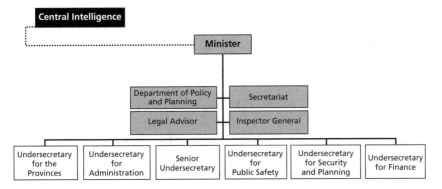

SOURCE: CPA.
NOTE: This structure was revised by later interim ministers in the spring of 2004. The insertion of "central intelligence" on the MoI organization chart in November 2003 was part of an attempt by CPA advisors to ensure that whichever intelligence services emerged would coordinate with but not be subordinate to the MoI.
RAND *MG365-3.2*

responsibility and local authority. Political direction and accountability were to be provided via the minister and his deputies in conjunction with provincial governors. Additional public accountability was to be provided through the use of local advisory councils. Public safety officials would have operational autonomy within a framework of national standards, policies, and oversight. This structure was designed to serve a number of principles that the CPA sought to imbue in the ministry, including

- Civilian primacy and oversight, which included separation of powers
- Operational command to be exercised by professional public safety officers
- A combination of centralized policy and standards, with decentralized operational control.

---

allow Iraqis to build a new country free from fear." CPA, *Ministry of Interior Organizational Plan*, November 2003.

In reconstructing and reforming the MoI, the CPA concentrated on a number of areas. First, it focused on the physical reconstruction of the ministry's facilities. Renovation and reconstruction were gradually completed in the fall of 2003 and spring of 2004. However, by June 2004, the ministry still lacked a communications infrastructure that would have enabled it to exercise real-time command and control over ministry operations countrywide. Second, the CPA introduced administrative reforms, including reform of financial management and personnel management systems, the civilianization of support functions, and the institution of anticorruption measures. The latter made some progress, with the development of a strong internal affairs department, but there was little progress in other areas. CPA MoI advisory staff and their Iraqi counterparts generally had to concentrate on short-term crisis management rather than on longer-term institutional development.

The Iraqi Police Service. Although U.S. prewar planning had envisaged relying on the IPS to keep order, the wholesale breakdown of law and order that followed the fall of Baghdad in April 2003 demonstrated the unreliability of this assumption. There were two central reasons the IPS did not function as expected. First, the decapitation of the Saddamist regime and the removal of the Ba'athist senior leadership that controlled the MoI left the IPS leaderless. Senior leaders either had fled or were removed during April and May 2003, prompting many of the junior personnel to follow suit. Although ORHA and coalition forces recalled Iraqi police personnel to work shortly after the fall of Baghdad, the militarized and hierarchical IPS did not operate effectively in a leadership vacuum.

Second, the IPS was not postured, trained, or equipped for the mission it was expected to undertake in the new Iraq. Under Saddam, internal security was the responsibility of a plethora of internal security agencies, supported when need be by formed military units, such as the Special Republican Guard. This network of organizations covered society with a comprehensive intelligence network and included secret police units with unbridled powers and armed units that could move quickly to stamp out incipient rebellions. The Iraqi police were relegated to a secondary status, left to deal with traffic offenses, street crime, and minor disputes. When the CPA formally abolished all the other Iraqi security institutions, the IPS was thrust into the front lines,[55] confronting organized, well-armed criminals and a sustained terrorist and insurgent campaign. It is very doubtful that any police force would have been able to cope with the levels of violence that erupted, let alone one as weak as the IPS.

Although early on, the CPA and CJTF-7 decided to make the IPS the primary Iraqi internal security agency and began a process of handing over responsibility for urban security to the force, neither the CPA, CJTF-7, Washington, nor London ever gave the IPS the priority it deserved. As late as June 2004, the IPS program was fighting for the resources and leadership that it required.

An initial assessment of the Iraqi police and justice system conducted by the CPA's International Police Assistance Team in May 2003 concluded that the Iraqi police were incapable of providing security and order.[56] The assessment noted that the police needed to be reconstituted so that they could perform immediate policing functions, as well as fundamentally transformed so that they could be both efficient and accountable.[57]

Coalition efforts to rebuild and transform Iraq's police can be understood by examining three aspects: transformation, politics and structure, and program delivery.

The CPA developed a twin-track approach to police transformation because there was an immediate need for police on the streets. This involved rehiring Saddam-era policemen and providing a minimal level of training in modern policing while beginning a full-scale recruitment and basic training program to bring new blood into the force. The intention of both programs was to produce a police force

---

[55] It would not have been politically or morally acceptable for the coalition to use the Saddam-era security organs, but the dissolution of these agencies created a foreseeable security vacuum.

[56] CPA, *Iraqi Police: An Assessment of the Present and Recommendations for the Future*, May 30, 2003.

[57] The difficulties the coalition faced were illustrated by the fact that members of the assessment team themselves were drawn into day-to-day management of the Baghdad police force.

with a wholly new culture—one of service to the community, dedicated to proactive policing and protection of civil liberties.

The first step was for CJTF-7 units, as the only international bodies with a presence outside Baghdad, to either rehire Saddam-era policemen or hire new policemen.[58] The CPA designed a three-week transition and integration training program. This was intended to verify the existence of police officers supposedly on the books,[59] to vet personnel, and to instill a modicum of modern policing skills and ethos.[60]

The absence of civilian police advisors outside Baghdad and Basra meant that much of the training was provided by military police units, usually operating through translators. Although these units often performed well, police training was only one of many missions they had. As well, they were teaching a civilian policing curriculum and had very limited knowledge of the culture and procedures already existing in the Iraqi criminal justice system. The quality of the personnel "rehired"[61] was also extremely variable. Even though by the summer of 2004, the actual number of serving police personnel was already at some 120,000 (30,000 above the target end-strength), this number included large numbers of personnel who were underage, past pensionable age, illiterate, or otherwise unfit for duty.

Longer-term transformation was to be achieved by gradually populating the force with new recruits brought in with much higher standards. These recruits were to go through an eight-week basic training course before embarking on a field-training program in

---

[58] The lack of records, most of which were looted or destroyed in April and May 2003, meant that it was very hard for CPA and other coalition officials to determine with any certainty who had been a serving IPS member before the war.

[59] As with other parts of the post-Saddam public sector, it appeared that many nominal employees were in fact "ghosts"—middlemen or officers often took pay for nonexistent personnel.

[60] Many Iraqi policemen lacked even basic skills. At least one coalition military police unit refused to issue extra ammunition to its local Iraqi police unit due to concerns about lack of firearms discipline.

[61] It subsequently emerged that many of the supposedly "rehired" officers in fact had no police experience at all.

which they would be supervised by coalition and Iraqi field-training officers.[62] This ambitious program involved an abortive attempt to undertake police training in Hungary, the construction of the Jordan International Police Training Center, and the build-out of the Baghdad Public Safety Academy and smaller training centers outside the capital. A vital part of the program was the planned deployment of international police advisors (IPAs) and international police trainers (IPTs).[63]

Although the initial focus of the police reform program was on training new recruits, it became increasingly clear that one of the primary weaknesses of the IPS was its senior leaders and managers. Some senior officers displayed great courage and dedication. Overall, however, the commitment and professional standards of the IPS leadership cadre were poor. This problem became particularly evident in April 2004 when the IPS in Fallujah, Mosul, Najaf, Karbala and other cities targeted by Sunni or Shi'ite insurgents melted away or went over to the insurgents. Subsequently, the police program was revamped to provide additional management and leadership training. Belatedly, a "train-the-trainer" program was instituted to free up scarce international resources to focus on working with the senior ranks.

The other leg of the police transformation program was the development of institutional capacity. This involved reorganizing the force, establishing specialized units, and educating the leadership. Reorganization had limited impact because of the IPS's resistance to

---

[62] The course was originally 12 weeks, but this was cut because of the requirement to rapidly deploy police officers to restore order.

[63] The numbers of IPAs and IPTs to be deployed underwent a series of revisions. An initial assessment in May 2003, based on the Balkans model, had called for up to 6,500 international personnel. By the fall of 2003, this had been revised to 1,500. In the spring of 2004, the target numbers were revised to 500 U.S. IPAs, 500 international IPAs, and 600 IPTs. None of these targets was anywhere near reached during the course of the CPA's existence. Although IPAs in Iraq were armed for self-defense, they did not have executive authority to enforce Iraqi law.

change,[64] but some progress was made on the establishment of specialized units. Training and equipping began in late spring of 2004 for such functions as criminal investigation, criminal intelligence, forensics, and such specialist subjects as terrorism, organized crime, drugs, and kidnapping. Leadership education also began in earnest in April 2004.

In addition to the reconstitution and transformation of the IPS, the CPA had to address the politics and the structure of the police. The politics of the police refers to the governance issues and the relations between police and society.[65] Structure refers specifically to the question of a "third force."[66]

In terms of politics, the CPA adopted an approach that was consistent with its overarching strategy of democratizing and decentralizing the Iraqi polity. The Saddam-era police force had been a national force tightly controlled by the interior ministry. In its training programs, the CPA sought to transform the attitudes of the IPS personnel and leadership into one of service to the community; it also took tentative steps to encourage local communities to seek oversight of their local police chiefs through public safety committees. In terms of national structure, however, CPA struggled with the tension between its desire to decentralize control so as to build a more accountable force and the requirement to retain central control to ensure effectiveness against insurgents and terrorists. In the end, the model chosen was a hybrid. Local police chiefs would have some autonomy but would be accountable both to the MoI in Baghdad and to local, elected councils and provincial governors.[67] National

---

[64] For instance, CPA advisors sought to change the structure of the Baghdad Police Department to bring together the separate "patrol" and "station" units, but the IPS officer corps successfully resisted this attack on established patterns of behavior.

[65] See David H. Bayley, *Patterns of Policing: A Comparative International Analysis*, New Brunswick, N.J.: Rutgers University Press, 1990, chapters 3 and 7, for comparative discussions of these topics.

[66] "Third force" refers to constabulary forces that lie somewhere between civilian police and armed forces

[67] CPA Order 71, Local Governmental Powers, April 6, 2004.

units, such as the Civil Intervention Force (CIF) outlined below, would operate under the authority of the central government but could be requested by local police chiefs.[68]

In terms of structure, there was a tension between making the IPS a community-based public safety force—the "cop on the beat"—and building it as a paramilitary organization, able to deal with high levels of organized crime and political violence. The CPA's civilian police advisors favored building a community-based police force that would, in the long run, build a democratic police force that would serve the citizens of Iraq. Other CPA advisors, however, favored emphasizing specialist, paramilitary police units able to take the fight to insurgents and terrorists. Iraqi police officers, coming from a tradition of colonial-style regime policing, were not averse to the latter approach.

Thus, although tentative efforts to promote community-policing initiatives were made, the CPA recognized that the IPS was always going to have something of a paramilitary flavor.[69] Nonetheless, there were long-running debates over the desirability of creating a wholly separate constabulary force, perhaps out of the ICDC. In early 2004, these proposals were rejected by the CPA's police advisors. Instead, they laid plans for the creation of specialized local and national police units to deal with "high-end" violence. These specialized national units became known as the Emergency Response Unit (an elite 270-man special weapons and tactics [SWAT] team) and the Civil Intervention Force (a 4,800-man national light-infantry-style force). These would be supplemented at local levels by public order units and more-conventional local police SWAT teams.[70] Although specialized,

---

[68] The three Kurdish provinces remained outside this system; the transitional administrative law gave them significant autonomy over policing.

[69] Initially, CPA officials resisted requests from the IPS that they be armed with heavier weapons to match the firepower of their opponents. By early summer of 2004, though, the violence had escalated to the point at which the IPS had to be routinely equipped with machine-guns.

[70] In the summer of 2004, Interior Minister Faleh Naqeeb rapidly and cheaply built and deployed several police "commando battalions" comprised of former special forces personnel. These units performed well in combat operations but bypassed the coalition-designed MoI

these units were intended be part of the Iraqi police, rather than constituting a wholly separate body.

As with all other areas of CPA activity, the plans and policies developed by the CPA suffered problems in the implementation phase. Program delivery proved to be a tremendous problem for the police sector. Design and implementation of the Iraqi police program fell to the U.S. government, primarily the State Department's Bureau of International Narcotics and Law Enforcement and the Justice Department's International Criminal Investigative Training Assistance Program. The United States deployed contractors and temporary hires into the Defense Department (known as "3161s"), supplemented by military personnel, to staff the police reform program.[71] They were assisted by the United Kingdom, Australia, Canada, and Spain, all of which deployed senior police officers to advise the Iraqi MoI. Other EU countries provided assistance with police training under UK auspices in the south of the country.[72]

Many of the U.S. government contractors and program managers had extensive experience with police reform from such operations as those in the Balkans and Haiti. However, the immediate security crisis meant that they had to effectively take over day-to-day police operations in many parts of the country. Although funds were allocated from the FY 2003 U.S. supplemental to enable the State Department to implement a police reform program, the resources available paled into insignificance given the size of the need. Even though significant financial resources began to become available in

---

chain of command, leading to some consternation amongst coalition advisors. Greg Jaffe, "New Factor in Iraq: Irregular Brigades Fill Security Void," *Wall Street Journal,* February 16, 2005.

[71] The contractors and 3161s had a wide variety of backgrounds. Some had many years of experience in police reform programs in the developing world; others were retired military or retired or serving police officers. Many of the younger staff had no relevant experience but partially made up for this with goodwill and enthusiasm.

[72] On UK perspectives, see UK House of Commons Defence Committee, *Oral Evidence of Dr Owen Greene, Chief Constable Paul Kernaghan, Mr Stephen Pattison and Mr Stephen Rimmer,* HC 65-i, January 26, 2005.

late 2003 from the Development Fund for Iraq (DFI)[73] and in spring 2004 from the FY 2004 U.S. supplemental, these funds took time to translate into contracts to provide personnel, equipment, or infrastructure on the ground. Moreover, the deteriorating security situation meant that the hoped-for international advisors did not materialize and those who did deploy were often very restricted in the extent to which they could work with their Iraqi counterparts.

Given this lack of a CPA footprint, even in key cities like Baghdad and Basra, CJTF-7 military police and civil affairs units were the main day-to-day liaison with the IPS. Despite their reluctance to get involved in civil policing, the military had to undertake the selection of leaders, oversee recruitment, provide basic training, and equip and mentor the police. Helped by the presence of police officers in U.S. reserve units, many of these efforts were remarkably successful.[74] But the attention that the military could give to the police was rudimentary, sporadic, and underfunded. It was also very uneven across the country. Moreover, because they had not been given the police mission, coalition forces often concentrated on building up the ICDC rather than supporting the police.

In March 2004, the U.S. Defense Department assessed progress made in developing the Iraqi security forces. The assessment noted that the police program was facing serious delays that would impair the ability of coalition forces to disengage from local security operations. It recommended transferring resources from the NIA program to the police and the ICDC and giving CJTF-7 the mission of developing the IPS since CPA lacked the required capacity. Although many of the CPA civilian advisors were wary of the concept of subordinating the police program to the military, the Defense Department concluded that only the military had the resources to move the

---

[73] DFI was established to manage Iraqi government assets and oil revenues under CPA direction during the occupation period. It subsequently transitioned to Iraqi government control, supervised by an international monitoring board.

[74] For instance, the organized crime unit operating out of Baquba police station in late 2003 and early 2004 scored notable successes.

police program forward fast enough to meet the deadline for transferring authority.

As a result, CJTF-7 established the Civilian Police Advisory Training Team. This team was under the operational control of CJTF-7 but took policy direction from CPA's MoI advisors. Headed by a military officer, with a civilian deputy, CPATT was staffed jointly by military and civilian personnel. It was given the mission of mobilizing civilian and military resources to staff, train, equip, and mentor the Iraqi police.[75]

CPATT's birth was difficult because of skepticism among many CPA civilian advisors about the wisdom of subordinating a civilian police program to the military. It was also baptized by fire, since it had to deal with the collapse of the IPS in Najaf and other southern cities during the April confrontation with insurgents even as it was trying to pull together its staff and other assets. Nonetheless, CPATT was probably a pragmatic recognition that, given the difficult circumstances of Iraq, civilian police advisors would have to rely on the military to help manage and deliver police reform and capacity-building.

IPS: Lessons and Implications. Reconstituting and reforming the IPS was a far more challenging task than any that previous U.S. or multinational nation-building missions had faced. Physically reconstituting the force so that it could carry out basic policing functions was hard enough; this task relied primarily on CJTF-7 military assets during the life of the CPA. Transforming the force into the lead public security agency in the face of unprecedented levels of violence and criminality while at the same time seeking to modernize and democratize the force was even more daunting. To undertake this mission with any expectation of success would have required a detailed understanding of the prewar IPS, along with the ability to rapidly mobilize reserves of money, equipment, and international police advisors. None of these was at hand during the life of CPA. Meanwhile, the

---

[75] With the transition from CJTF-7 to MNF-I in May 2004, CPATT became part of the Office of Security Transition (OST), which was renamed in June the Multinational Security Transition Command–Iraq (MNSTC-I), the MNF-I office charged with responsibility for manning, training, and equipping all Iraqi security forces.

deteriorating security situation bloodied the nascent police service while slowing the deployment of international advisors as well as the implementation of vital infrastructure projects, such as the police communications network.

Some of the lessons from the IPS experience are familiar from other nation-building operations.[76] First, it is not unusual for the police force of a centralized autocracy to collapse once the regime is changed, nor is it unusual for widespread looting to take place. Second, it always takes time to mobilize and deploy international police advisors, whether CIVPOL in a UN mission or contractors in the U.S. model. It is always difficult to persuade home departments and police forces to give up their good people for extended tours. This inevitably leaves a security gap in which the international military forces, if possible assisted by constabulary units,[77] need to take on the policing role. Third, organized crime targeted at local citizens and infrastructures flourishes in transitional states. If not targeted early on by international military and police forces, it can destabilize reconstruction and democratization efforts. Fourth, unless the police force is being rebuilt from the ground up, as in Kosovo, then it is important to work with and through local institutions rather than seeking to import wholesale Western models. These will inevitably be subverted as the local institutions revert to their standard modes of operating.

Some of the particular lessons relate to flaws in program implementation by the coalition. In the critical first year of the occupation, the coalition did not give the police program the priority it deserved. It suffered from inadequate personnel and financial resources and an

---

[76] James Burack, William Lewis, and Edward Marks, *Civilian Police and Multinational Peacekeeping—A Workshop Series: A Role for Democratic Policing*, Washington D.C.: National Institute of Justice, October 6, 1997 (published January 1999); Robert B. Oakley, Michael J. Dziedzic, and Eliot M. Goldberg, eds., *Policing the New World Disorder: Peace Operations and Public Security*, Washington, D.C.: National Defense University Press, 1998; Annika S. Hansen, *From Congo to Kosovo: Civilian Police in Peace Operations*, Adelphi Paper 343, London: International Institute for Strategic Studies, 2002.

[77] Robert M. Perito, *Where Is the Lone Ranger When We Need Him? America's Search for a Postconflict Stability Force*, Washington, D.C.: United States Institute of Peace, 2004.

ambivalent level of support from CJTF-7. The CPA was slow to recognize that policing had to be at the top of its priorities, but when it did it found that the U.S. State Department was unable to deliver the number of police trainers required and that CJTF-7 was focused more on supporting the ICDC and the NIA than the IPS.

The resultant staff shortages meant that the police advisors in Iraq spent most of their time managing MoI and IPS operations rather than engaging in institutional development and capacity-building. Furthermore, even when security had risen up the CPA's list of priorities, the authority chose not to fully fund all security-related projects, such as the identification card program and passport systems, believing that continued investment in social welfare and infrastructures was an equally important priority. Second, the police program suffered from a number of midcourse corrections. Some of these were no doubt worthwhile,[78] but the overall impact was to divert effort from fulfillment of the ongoing plans.

In terms of implications for the future, the MoI and IPS programs remain in a critical state. While U.S. supplemental funds are now flowing, allowing equipment to be procured and distributed and training programs to be expanded, shortages of international advisors both in the staff of CPATT and MoI and in the IPA and IPT programs will continue to delay the building of Iraqi capacity. Increasing the raw numbers of police on the streets is no substitute for developing institutional capacity and building a high-quality, efficient, accountable police service. The IPS's main advantage at present is the relatively high regard in which it is held by the Iraqi public; maintaining and building on this respect to ensure genuine community support will be the key to the success of the police.[79]

Population, Border, and Weapons Control. In addition to delivering urban and rural policing, the interior ministry was tasked with implementing border and population control.

---

[78] For example, the refocus on leadership and specialist training in spring 2004.

[79] See, for instance, International Republican Institute, *Survey of Iraqi Public Opinion, December 26, 2004–January 7, 2005*, Washington, D.C., 2005.

Iraq's borders under Saddam had been protected by a large conscript force of more than 100,000 men but had never been secure against smugglers and infiltrators. In August 2003, the CPA reorganized border control assets from various ministries (Interior, Defense, and Finance) into a single Department of Border Enforcement (DBE) under the MoI.[80] The DBE was given responsibility for border policing as well as customs, the development of a new passport system, and immigration functions.[81] Since the majority of the personnel previously employed in these tasks had either deserted or been dismissed because of their association with the Ba'ath Party or the intelligence services, most staff had to be recruited and trained anew. At the same time, most border facilities had been ruined in the war or from looting. As with the IPS, the DBE program was implemented by a handful of coalition personnel—some drawn from specialist agencies in the United States or United Kingdom, others drawn from the ranks of U.S. Army civil affairs units.[82] In the meantime, coalition forces had responsibility for securing Iraq's borders. The fact that they lacked the resources to effectively control the borders was evident from the widespread smuggling, infiltration, and other cross-border traffic such as returning refugees from Iran.

Population control measures, such as identity cards, passports, weapons permits, and security vetting, were programs for which the interior and foreign ministries shared responsibility. Coalition advisors and their Iraqi counterparts found themselves hamstrung by the loss of most central government files and databases, although certain records, such as army personnel records and the food ration card database, provided a basis on which to build. However, despite numerous initiatives to deploy the latest database and biometric technologies, by the time of the transfer of authority the CPA had failed

---

[80] CPA Order 26, Creation of the Department of Border Enforcement, August 24, 2003.

[81] The CPA initially planned the DBE to be 18,000 strong, which was clearly inadequate in light of the length of Iraq's borders.

[82] The challenges this program faced were highlighted when the U.S. Department of Homeland Security decided in February 2004 not to assign customs staff to Iraq because of security concerns.

to resource or implement comprehensive and effective population control measures.

Weapons control also encompassed control of Iraq's vast ammunition storage sites. Control of these sites and disposal of arms and munitions were the responsibility of CJTF-7, which handed over disposal operations to contractors in a phased process. Over time, the most accessible sites and the most likely sources of insurgent arms did come under more control by the coalition and of ISF. However, a lack of military resources meant that these dumps remained a prime source of insurgent materiel beyond the life of the CPA.

Population, Border, and Weapons Control: Lessons and Implications. Border, population, and weapons control were vital to the improvement of the Iraqi security situation, although full-scale disarmament of the population was never feasible. The coalition confronted the mammoth task of constructing such control mechanisms as border forces, physical and electronic infrastructures, and databases. Although CJTF-7 undertook some of these tasks, it had neither the forces nor the funds to implement more than piecemeal approaches. The CPA failed to prioritize these tasks; it applied few resources to these problems and moved surprisingly slowly on key elements, such as population and weapons registration and visas.

The implications for future Iraqi governments are that, while they urgently need to enhance border security, population, and weapons control measures, they will have to do so through an MoI that lacks capacity. Fortunately, many of these problems can be fixed —at least in the medium term—by the provision of external financial or technical assistance and training.

The Justice Sector

Justice sector reform has often been the poor stepchild of security sector reform. In many cases, strong police forces and militaries have been built, but a weak judiciary has meant that the rule of law is undermined either by the state security forces or by organized crime and corruption.[83] This was recognized by the CPA, which initiated a significant program to overhaul the Iraqi judicial and prisons system in the summer of 2003. Indeed, in October 2003, the case was explicitly made in an internal CPA report that "the holistic reform of the criminal justice sector is vital to the building of durable security capacity. It is important to ensure that the justice and policing systems develop together and are mutually reinforcing."[84] However, the program was hampered by delays in the deployment of resources in terms of funds and civilian advisors.

Judicial and prison reform were the responsibility of the U.S. Department of Justice, supported by U.S. Army civil affairs and Judge Advocate General officers. As with the IPS, the bulk of the work on the ground with Iraqi prisons or courts was undertaken by CJTF-7.

The CPA implemented sweeping reforms of the judicial and correctional system. Early CPA orders transferred responsibility for prisons to the Ministry of Justice (MoJ), laid the basis for an independent judiciary, and reformed the penal code. Although the courts and judiciary had been politicized and subordinated to the intelligence services and Ba'ath Party, Iraq had a body of judges and prosecutors who were relatively honest, educated, and professional. Within a short time, most of Iraq's courthouses were functioning and serious work had begun on reforming Iraq's penal code. By 2004, judges had been vetted; those thought to be corrupt or guilty of human rights abuses removed from their posts; and others, dismissed by Saddam, reappointed.

In reality, the Iraqi judiciary were a long way from being effective. Fears over their security made most judges reluctant to investigate or try the more serious cases. Three judges were murdered in November 2003, prompting emergency efforts to provide judges with bodyguards. There was little urgency among judges about processing

---

[83] Goran Hyden, Julius Court, and Kenneth Mease, *Making Sense of Governance*, Boulder, Colo.: Lynne Rienner, 2004, chapter 8.

[84] CPA, *Security Sector Synchronization Exercise Outbrief*, October 11, 2003.

cases, and it was common for suspects to remain in police custody for weeks without appearing before the court. Lack of nationwide communications meant that many courts received new legislation from Baghdad weeks or even months after it had been passed.

The situation in Iraq's prisons was worse. Although the CPA consolidated Iraq's prisons under the MoJ in an attempt to reduce the scope of abuses under the interior and labor ministries, this program ran into bureaucratic wrangling between the police and corrections services. The vast majority of Iraqi Corrections Service officers were completely unfit to work in a modern prison service. Recruits and managers had to be found, trained, and mentored. The physical infrastructure of the Iraqi prisons system, inadequate before the war, was comprehensively looted in the conflict's aftermath. The CPA initiated a program of prisons refurbishment and building, but its original budget request for some $400 million for this task was reduced to approximately $100 million as the FY 2004 U.S. supplemental passed through Congress.

Confronting Organized Crime and Corruption. The CPA also recognized that two longer-term issues had to be addressed. First, the justice and police systems had to be given the capabilities to deal with serious organized crime and terrorism as well as ordinary crime. This would require judicial-police units with the dedication, skills, and resources (as well as the courage) to tackle these threats. Only small steps were taken in this direction.

Second, the new Iraq had to tackle endemic corruption. In January 2004, the Commission on Public Integrity was launched.[85] This was set up as an independent investigative commission that would focus on major cases of corruption. At the same time, all Iraqi ministries were instructed to appoint an Inspector General and a

---

[85] CPA, "Commission on Public Integrity to Combat Government Corruption," press release, January 31, 2004.

staff.[86] Further oversight was provided by the reconstitution of Iraq's Board of Supreme Audit, an independent supervisory body.[87]

Judicial Systemic Reform. The focus of the CPA's judicial reform efforts was to institutionalize the independence of the judiciary. The Council of Judges, abolished by Saddam in 1979, was reestablished in September 2003. The council was separated from the MoJ and given authority over court budgets, personnel, security, and property.[88] In addition, the CPA established the Central Criminal Court of Iraq with nationwide jurisdiction and a mandate to concentrate on the more serious crimes with which other courts were often reluctant to deal, such as terrorism and organized crime.[89] Work was also initiated to assist in the establishment of an Iraqi Supreme Court.

Justice Sector: Lessons and Implications. Metrics for judicial effectiveness, for instance time from detention to trial and throughput of cases, were collected on an ad hoc basis by coalition military lawyers and the CPA's MoJ advisors, but as of June 2004 the Iraqi Council of Judges had been unable to institute a routine data collection procedure to allow it to monitor judicial performance. Nonetheless, the final assessments of the CPA's judicial advisors in June 2004 indicated that the Iraqi judicial system had much further to go.[90]

More fundamental problems with the Iraqi justice system were revealed in advisors' statements that even the Central Criminal Court of Iraq, established to handle the more difficult cases, was severely hampered by the weaknesses of the investigative agencies. As MoJ

---

[86] CPA Order 57, Iraqi Inspectors General, February 10, 2004.

[87] CPA Order 77, Board of Supreme Audit, April 25, 2004.

[88] CPA Order 35, Re-Establishment of the Council of Judges, September 15, 2003.

[89] CPA Order 13, The Central Criminal Court of Iraq (Amended), April 22, 2004.

[90] By June 2003, the CPA had set a detention to trial target of one month, but it was only able to move toward achievement of this target in Baghdad by sending its Judicial Assessment and Reconstruction Team to review some 2,000 cases of criminal and security detainees, computerizing Baghdad's courts, developing a prisoner transportation plan for Baghdad, and training police investigators on interrogation techniques and criminal procedures. CPA, *Strategic Plan,* June 25, 2004.

advisors noted, "law-enforcement agencies are too easily intimidated."[91] There remained a pressing need for specialized investigative teams made up of police and judicial officials able to resist the pressures of violence and corruption that hampered the imposition of rule of law in Iraq.[92]

The CPA's justice and prisons programs suffered from the same failings as other areas—shortages of and delays in the supply of funding, equipment, and expatriate personnel. The deteriorating security situation from the spring of 2004 also reduced the ability of the CPA to mentor and support the justice sector. For instance, early CPA plans had called for the deployment of international advisors in each province to assist the local courts. This program had to be scrapped in the spring of 2004 because of the difficulty of deploying civilian teams into insecure areas and the inability of the military to resource the effort.

The implications of a weak judicial and prisons sector for the rule of law under future Iraqi governments are dire. Previous nation-building cases have demonstrated that, even if professional police and armed forces are created, a weak judicial and prison system will undermine progress toward the rule of law, which in turn will harm public safety, democratization, and economic growth.

Infrastructure Security

Infrastructure security was recognized as a problem in the immediate aftermath of the postwar looting. This looting was superseded during 2003 by increasingly organized and widespread sabotage and criminality directed against Iraq's infrastructure. Threats ranged from insurgent bombings of oil pipelines and railroads to attacks on aircraft to criminal theft of electrical wires to hijackings of trucks. Coalition forces, the ICDC, and police were deployed against these threats, but a range of infrastructure security forces were also created. One of these forces, the Facilities Protection Service (FPS), was made up of

---

[91] CPA, *Strategic Plan,* June 25, 2004.

[92] *Quarterly Report to Congress,* 2207 report, July 2004.

minimally trained static guards. The Ministry of Interior had over-sight for training and policy purposes, but each line ministry con-trolled and funded its own FPS contingent, which was controlled and funded by its parent ministries.[93] Ministries with greater resources and particular vulnerabilities, such as oil and electricity, contracted out security provision to foreign or local private security companies.[94]

Infrastructure Security: Lessons and Implications. The rate of attacks on critical infrastructure and the damage these have caused to the reconstruction program show that neither CJTF-7 nor ISF have managed to control the problem. Furthermore, some steps that were taken, such as paying tribes to protect pipelines and road routes, may have contributed to the problem. Nonetheless, certain important ini-tiatives did help ameliorate the risks. These included the training of professional security forces for the oil ministry, deployment of rapid repair teams, the planned use of the IAF air wing for infrastructure surveillance, and creation of coalition coordination centers to assist contractors.

For the future, aside from continuing to build quality ISF and ensuring good coordination, improving infrastructure security will rely heavily on improved intelligence gathering at the local level. The IPS will play the key role here. In the meantime, the Iraqi govern-ment has initiated a plan to build and deploy specialized army units for infrastructure security.

The Intelligence Services

One of the CPA's first acts had been to abolish the myriad Iraqi intelligence services. Unfortunately, formal abolition of the structures was not the same as uprooting their networks. It was these networks that facilitated the upsurge of insurgent and criminal activity; with skills sharpened over many years, the underground remnants of the

---

[93] The FPS spun off a number of specialist subunits, such as the Diplomatic Protection Ser-vice, which serviced foreign embassies and international missions in Iraq.

[94] The MoI had the responsibility for regulating private security companies, which pro-liferated in occupied Iraq, but the regulation process remained ad hoc during the life of the CPA.

Saddam-era intelligence apparatus were always ahead of the coalition in their ability to gather information and to intimidate the population.

Although building reformed Iraqi intelligence structures was part of the ORHA planning mandate, CPA officials initially felt that the issue of secret services was best left to a future Iraqi government. The history of oppression suggested that Iraqis might benefit from a hiatus without such structures.

In the meantime, however, the CIA and its British counterparts had been tasked with and began work on the creation of an Iraqi intelligence structure. They focused on ensuring that the organization could acquire and process intelligence effectively to support coalition activities in Iraq. In addition, it became clear that both the MoI and MoD would have some intelligence capabilities of their own. Furthermore, the U.S. 1st Armored Division in Baghdad created an Iraqi intelligence cell of its own, which supported CJTF-7's intelligence efforts. Thus, Iraqi intelligence structures were emerging. Without oversight, they would continue to develop independently of each other, creating dangers of stovepiping, competing services, and, quite possibly, abuse.

If any organization in the CPA were to oversee the process of building intelligence agencies, it would have to be the Office of Security Affairs. In line with this, that office requested an intelligence specialist and received one staff member in October 2003. While the CPA was able to establish that it had a role to play in this process, the creation of the Iraqi National Intelligence Service was clearly in the hands of the CIA and British intelligence; CPA staff had limited visibility into their planning and actions until the CIA briefed the concept for the INIS to the CPA in November 2003. The INIS was described as focused on domestic intelligence collection and analysis, without a substantial foreign mission.

CPA's OSA, whose mandate covered the overall design of the Iraqi national security architecture, in which the INIS would be only one component, recognized the need to create an overarching, coordinating structure for intelligence efforts. The immediate focus of those building the INIS, however, was on getting an operational entity up and running—not ensuring that it could fit into a still-evolving design. Because the CIA was not organizationally subordinated to the CPA, initial efforts in late 2003 to assert oversight by the CPA were not successful. Early in 2004, the effort was reengaged, driven in large part by the requirement to introduce the INIS to the IGC and to receive approval of the organization's charter. This process also brought to light a number of critical issues regarding Iraq's intelligence services.

One of the issues in question was that of detention authority for the INIS. While some felt that the INIS ought to be able to arrest and interrogate suspects, others thought that, given Iraq's history of abusive intelligence services, it was best that arrest and detention be left to the police. Another issue was the hiring of former members of Iraqi intelligence services to staff the INIS. IGC members were concerned that the INIS would recreate old oppressive structures. In addition, the creation of the INIS brought to the surface questions of the roles of the MoI and MoD in creating and overseeing intelligence capabilities, relations between the various agencies, and the integration of Iraqi intelligence functions developed by coalition forces.

These issues moved onto the agenda of the CPA's Security Institutions Steering Group and were debated by senior advisors and officials for several months in the spring of 2004. They were also discussed with senior Iraqi personnel through the Security Committee of the IGC. In the end, it was decided that the INIS would have no arrest or detention authority, that the hiring of former Iraqi intelligence staff would be minimized, and that the involvement of such personnel would diminish over time.[95]

In terms of architectures, a distributed model was agreed upon. The INIS would work closely with the Ministry of Interior, via a Special Branch–type relationship, to ensure that arrest and detention took place as needed on the basis of INIS information. The INIS would also be the "first among equals" of intelligence agencies, coordinating policy and analysis among them. On April 1, 2004, the IGC

---

[95] The CPA had no effective means to verify that these decisions were implemented, and anecdotal evidence suggests they were honored in the breach.

was authorized to create the INIS by issuing a charter for that organization, which it promptly did. The interim director general of the INIS was appointed on April 4.[96]

However, unresolved issues remained. MoD intelligence, in accordance with the CPA order that created the ministry, had a role in analysis. Its analytical work was to focus on foreign threats, and it was to have no collection capacity, but this created a challenge because no Iraqi agency was explicitly tasked with external collection.[97] The relationship between the INIS and the MoI also remained unclear. No progress was made on putting the Special Branch model into practice, although the MoI's criminal intelligence capability developed gradually.

Since the transfer of authority, the intelligence structure has appeared increasingly stovepiped and confusing, particularly given statements by Prime Minister Allawi that he planned to recreate the General Security Directorate, with its own arrest and detention capacity.[98] It is evident that the MoD and MoI continue to develop their own intelligence functions separately and that MoD plans to set up a collection department. This is not in itself a problem. Concerns arise, however, in the failure to institutionalize a coordinated intelligence community. Despite efforts by Iraqis and their coalition advisors, the short-term need to get structures up and running was seen as more crucial than ensuring that these structures worked well together.

Intelligence: Lessons and Implications. The CPA made two mistakes in this field: one of omission, the other of commission. The mistake of omission was to stay out of the intelligence sector until it was too late to ensure that the INIS and other intelligence structures could be built in a transparent and coordinated manner, in keeping

---

[96] The director was Mohammed Abdullah Mohammed al-Shehwani, an ethnic Turkmen who had lost two sons to Saddam's security services.

[97] The INIS charter states that the service will "collect, analyze and disseminate" information relating to "terrorism, domestic insurgency, espionage, narcotics production and trafficking, weapons of mass destruction, serious organized crime and other issues related to the national defense or threats to Iraqi democracy ...." INIS Charter, issued by the IGC, April 2, 2004.

[98] "Allawi Creates Iraq Anti-Terror Force," MSNBC News, July 15, 2004.

with the institutional needs of Iraq as a whole. Moreover, by allowing organizations not in the CPA chain of command to develop the INIS in its early stages with little input from outside its ranks, the CPA lost much of the initiative in defining the future of Iraqi intelligence. If CPA had established oversight on intelligence development early and retained it throughout, the development of a new security service would probably have proceeded more efficaciously. It might have been possible to build more rational, interdependent institutions, perhaps even with more of an eye to Iraqi needs.

The mistake of commission was to design but not effectively implement a distributed intelligence architecture. A centralized secret police agency may have been more effective in the short term in dealing with the insurgencies, but the CPA rejected this model to provide a sounder basis for a democratically accountable intelligence community. To make this model work, however, required active coalition support for the creation of key capabilities, such as an MoI Special Branch, and trust and cooperation between Iraqi ministries. Neither commodity was available.

Disarmament, Demobilization, and Reintegration

DDR has been a standard feature of most nation-building operations and is generally regarded as a necessary condition for the transition to sustainable peace.[99] In Iraq, DDR was conceived as two distinct programs: DDR of former Iraqi military personnel, and transition and reintegration (TR) of armed opposition groups.[100]

As discussed above, CENTCOM planning had included an assumption that members of the Iraqi military would be put through a DDR process after the conclusion of major combat operations. A comprehensive and costly program was outlined to ORHA by the

---

[99] Dahrendorf (2003), pp. 37–38. See also James Dobbins, John G. McGinn, Keith Crane, Seth G. Jones, Rollie Lal, Andrew Rathmell, Rachel Swanger, and Anga Timilsina, *America's Role in Nation-Building: From Germany to Iraq*, Santa Monica, Calif.: RAND Corporation, MR-1753-RC, 2003.

[100] The term TR was developed by the CPA in the face of opposition by the militias to the use of the term "disarmament."

Ronco Corporation in March 2003. More detailed plans for a pilot scheme to set up three DDR centers for former military personnel were considered by ORHA in April and May 2003.[101] However, by the time that Bremer and Slocombe deployed to the CPA in May 2003, the effective self-demobilization of the Iraqi armed forces made a formal DDR process unworkable and unnecessary. Instead, during the summer of 2003 a stipend program for former military personnel was developed, which paid thousands of Iraqi veterans. Although protests by former soldiers and officers took place during the latter half of 2003, the payments and the recruitment of former military personnel for the new security forces addressed some of the concerns of former Iraqi officers. In the last months of the CPA, a Veterans Agency was also established, and the Ministry of Labor and Social Affairs job training and placement program was in part targeted at former soldiers.

The question of a DDR process for Iraq's militias did, however, become of increasing concern in late 2003. From the outset, elimination of Iraq's militias had been a nominal coalition goal. However, until December 2003, when the November 15 agreement concentrated efforts, no substantive action was taken.[102] The CPA did seek to reduce the size of the Kurdish peshmerga but decided that dealing with the militias was not a high priority. Instead, coalition military units made tactical arrangements with militias on an ad hoc basis.[103]

---

[101] Ronco Corporation, "Decision Brief to Department of Defense Office of Reconstruction and Humanitarian Assistance on the Disarmament, Demobilization and Reintegration of the Iraqi Armed Forces," March 2003.

[102] Indeed, in November 2003, the CPA Executive Board was informed that "the original CPA objective to DDR sub-state militias may no longer be feasible. Offensive actions will continue against non-compliant militias. Compliant militias may however be integrated into the Iraqi security sector. If this approach is adopted, however, it should be on the basis of a clear political-security strategy rather than as an ad hoc response to short-term operational requirements." CPA, *Security Sector Reform: An Example of Structures Designed for Counter-Insurgency and for the Transition*, November 29, 2004.

[103] For instance, CJTF-7 put in place an intelligence-sharing arrangement with five of the main militias, and CJTF-7 units in the north relied on the Kurdish peshmerga to undertake policing and border security operations.

Once CPA decided to tackle this issue in the spring of 2004, it produced a comprehensive TR strategy. The essence of this strategy was to persuade former resistance forces[104] to undergo transition and reintegration through an approach that included:

- Determining which resistance forces could be reached by political or other diplomatic efforts and working with them to reach agreements
- Establishing the civil-military coordination essential for ensuring a successful program
- Using TR plans to draw down former resistance groups over a reasonable amount of time
- Transferring responsibility to the IIG prior to July 1, 2004.

This effort took place in a unique post-conflict situation. The organizations to be disbanded were not enemy fighters but in some very real ways allies of the coalition. A delicate balance therefore had to be struck between the security needs of a viable country and the respect due to those who fought Saddam. Additionally, the CPA approach acknowledged two fundamental points. First, the character of the new central government would not be known until after the constitution has been written and a permanent government elected. This will determine whether these groups will disband permanently. Second, Iraq's ethnic, religious, and tribal divisions will play a significant role in the willingness of Iraq's communities to disband their armed forces.

Of the several former resistance forces in Iraq, three were pivotal, owing to their size and connection to important Iraqi political parties: the peshmergas of the Patriotic Union of Kurdistan (PUK) and the Kurdistan Democratic Party (KDP), and the Badr Organiza-

---

[104] The term "militia" was used sparingly. Instead, the policy refers to "resistance forces" when we need one term to indicate all former armed forces and militias. While the term militia is appropriate for many of the forces, the peshmerga are professional armies. The term "former resistance force" or "resistance force" refers to those who fought in the resistance against Saddam Hussein and his Ba'athist regime. As used here, it also includes militias that were created after the conflict with the Ba'athist regime.

tion of the Supreme Council for the Islamic Revolution in Iraq (SCIRI). All other resistance forces were either smaller but politically important (primarily those whose leaders were members of the IGC), relatively large but unreachable by political means (e.g. Jaish al-Mahdi and former regime elements), or small and politically less important. None who would work inside the political process was denied an opportunity to participate.

The result of the TR program was that, by June 28, 2004, the CPA had agreements in place to provide the nine most significant "compliant"[105] militias, numbering some 102,000 fighters, with a legal status that would allow their members to transition into government security forces or reintegrate into civil society through retirement or job training and placement programs.[106] TR plans were in place and accepted by each of the nine groups, along with detailed implementation schedules.[107]

The CPA did not apply significant extra funding to implementing the TR program.[108] Rather, the intention was that most of the fighters were to be absorbed by existing programs. Three tracks were developed to provide new opportunities for former resistance fighters:

1. Transition into security forces, managed by MNF-I
2. Retirement for those eligible; facilitated by the creation of the Iraqi Veterans Agency

---

[105] That is, those not engaged in military activities against the coalition.

[106] The nine were the Patriotic Union of Kurdistan, Kurdistan Democratic Party, Badr Corps, Iraqi Communist Party, Iraqi Hezbollah, Iraqi Islamic Party, Iraqi National Accord, Iraqi National Congress, and al–Da'awa (Jaffari faction). Several other militias expressed interest in participating in the TR process, including the 15th Shabban and Sahid al-Shuhada as well as another faction of the Da'awa party. The Mujahidin e-Khalq and Kadek, considered foreign terrorist groups, were outside the process of TR.

[107] The authoritative documents on the TR strategy and law are the CPA's *Transition and Reintegration Strategy*, May 2004, and CPA Order 91, Regulation of Armed Forces and Militias Within Iraq, June 2004. They provide a comprehensive description of the effort and the law.

[108] The effort was unfunded and all but unstaffed as late as the start of 2004. In the spring of 2004, the CPA TR office was one person strong.

3. Vocational training and job placement programs for those not taking one of the first two tracks.

Oversight of the TR effort, initially under coalition control, was transferred to the IIG's interministerial Transition and Reintegration Implementation Committee (TRIC) by the end of June 2004. However, the TRIC was ineffective under the IIG, due in large part to the fact that its chairman, a representative of the MoI, had neither the confidence of his own minister nor of the prime minister.[109]

Interministerial committees, alone and unaided, are not well suited for running important programs. To support the TRIC, an office was proposed that would be staffed by international DDR experts and assisted by Iraqi staff. As the TR program office, its functions would include making sure that the TRIC was aware of political issues that needed resolution and running the support efforts needed to move former fighters into one of the three tracks. As part of a policy of avoiding new, open-ended financial commitments as the date for transfer of authority to the IIG drew near, the CPA declined to fund this effort in late May and early June 2004.[110] The Iraqi Ministry of Finance did not pursue the program.[111]

Because not all former fighters could move into a track at once, there was to be a period during which, from a legal perspective, the armed organization would cease to exist, and be considered a "residual element" of its previous self.[112] These residual elements were to be controlled by the MoI, in consultation with MNF-I, operating under a UN Security Council mandate. As of this writing, the MoI has not

---

[109] The change of ministers that took place with the transition from the CPA to the IIG led to the replacement of the defense and interior ministers who embraced the TR strategy with two who did not support it.

[110] The request was for approximately $10 million over 18 months.

[111] The CPA recommended that the U.S. embassy establish a TR support office, but the State Department declined to take on this mission.

[112] "Residual element" was the legal category devised to allow the coalition and then the IIG to declare all militias illegal, while giving those that agreed to disband time to do so in a controlled manner that included transition programs for their members.

put in place a mechanism to undertake this arrangement. This is significant because, although they are nominally signed up to a TR process, the nine militias since the end of the CPA have effectively continued to operate as autonomous, non-state armed forces.

Furthermore, according to the CPA TR plan, coalition countries were to continue to advise and provide resources, along with international donors and international organizations. This would have involved the creation of appropriate coordination mechanisms. However, because of staff limitations and other priorities, coalition embassies and missions have given little to no attention to this effort.

DDR: Lessons and Implications. Although the CPA and CJTF-7 had made DDR of the armed forces and dissolution of militias one of their policy goals from the outset, they decided not to implement a comprehensive strategy and failed to resource the militia TR process when this was initiated. As a result, progress in transitioning former fighters into the security forces was only beginning to be evident at the end of June 2004.[113] At least some of the problems with Sunni disaffection can be traced to this failure to reintegrate the Sunni army officer corps, whether into the new security forces or into other positions.

Since June 2004, neither the IIG nor the international diplomatic or military leadership has made DDR or TR a priority. Leadership, coordination, and resourcing are all lacking, meaning that the militia TR effort in Iraq has effectively ceased. This has clear implications for the ability of the Iraqi state to exercise a monopoly of force. While all of the nine militias engaged in the TR process are generally supporting the current political process, they retain their personnel and arms and hence the option to resort to force.

To resurrect the TR effort, the Iraqi government will first have to secure political agreement from the militia leaders that they remain committed to the TR process. If agreement is reaffirmed, then the TR program will require management and resourcing. Specifically:

---

[113] Recruiting into the IAF began in April 2004. By June, all militia groups had been through at least two rounds of recruiting for the IAF, with a schedule in place to fulfill all pledges made by the CPA to them.

- *Iraqi government*: The TRIC needs to be reconstituted and led by an MoI or MoD representative at the deputy minister level, reporting directly to the deputy prime minister for security. The chair needs to renegotiate TR agreements with all groups, since the agreed-on time schedules are no longer viable. The prime minister needs to personally support this effort and ensure that tracks 1 and 3, effectively eliminated by the ministers of defense and labor and social affairs, are reinstated.
- *International support*: The international community needs to support TRIC with a donor assistance committee to provide policy and fiscal support to the Iraqi-led effort to disband the militias.

CHAPTER FOUR

Evaluating Security Sector Reform in Iraq

In this chapter, we provide an evaluation of the coalition's security sector reform efforts during the tenure of the CPA. We start by summarizing developments in the security situation in Iraq and then assess the state of the various elements of the security sector at the time of transition of authority. We then identify six underlying problems with the coalition's approaches; these provide broader lessons from the CPA experience. We conclude with some recommendations for future priorities in the Iraq SSR program.

Evolution of the Security Situation, May 2003–June 2004

Most of the CPA and CJTF-7's measures of developments in the Iraqi security sector related to security inputs (e.g., money spent, equipment provided) and outputs (e.g., recruited and trained ISF personnel, units formed). The more important measures from the perspective of achieving U.S., Iraqi, and partner national security goals are security outcomes.[1] The fundamental question is whether

---

[1] This categorization of inputs, outputs, and outcomes has been developed at greater length in a RAND study on post-conflict policing. That study defines the terms as follows:

Inputs refer to the amount of resources used in reconstructing internal security, such as the amount of financial assistance provided and international personnel deployed. The amounts used, not the amounts budgeted, are the most relevant numbers.... Outputs refer to completed work, such as the number of police and military personnel trained. Finally, outcomes refer to conditions that directly affect the public, such as crime rates or perception of the rule of law. Outcomes are

enough progress is being made toward creating the security and rule-of-law conditions that are necessary to underpin political transition and economic development. Measuring levels of internal security and rule of law provided by a country's security sector is hard. Nonetheless, aggregate measures of security and rule of law combining levels of political violence, crime, corruption, and perceptions of public safety have been developed. Unfortunately, accurate and up-to-date assessments for Iraq are not available.[2] Instead, we can use proxy indicators, such as the level of political violence, crime, and public perceptions of security.

The publicly available quantitative data on political violence and crime indicate a negative trend. Attacks against coalition forces and civilian administrators and contractors have increased in number and sophistication since the summer of 2003. There has also been a significant upward trend in attacks on Iraqi civilians and officials (see Figure 4.1).

The partial data available (from Baghdad) on "ordinary" crime (murders and major property crimes) support the public perception of a dramatic increase in such crimes since April 2003. Although major property crimes have declined since their peak in the summer of 2003, as Table 4.1 shows, the same cannot be said of reported homicides.

Perceptions of security among Iraqi citizens more or less match the trends in reported crimes and attacks. Polls indicate that security and public safety were of even greater concern in May 2004 than they had been in January, when they were already the top priority. There was growing concern at the civilian toll taken by terrorist attacks, but

---

not what governments and international institutions do, but represent the consequences of their efforts.

Seth G. Jones, Jeremy M. Wilson, Andrew Rathmell, and K. Jack Riley, *Establishing Law and Order After Conflict*, Santa Monica, Calif.: RAND Corporation, MG-374-RC, 2005, p. 178.

[2] The World Bank governance indicators are an example of such measures. World Bank, Governance Indicators, 1996–2004, 2005.

Figure 4.1
Iraqi Civilian and U.S. Casualties

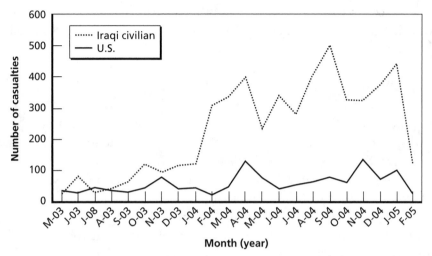

SOURCES: Compiled from Brookings Institution, Iraq Index; Iraq Coalition Casualty
Count; and Iraq Body Count Project.
RAND MG365-4.1

Table 4.1
Annualized Crime Rates per 100,000 Population

Period	Murder	Major Crime
2003 (May–December)	23.3	61.6
2004 (January–April)	31.5	50.2

SOURCES: Crime data supplied by the Baghdad Police Department. Baghdad population data supplied by the Iraqi Central
Statistical Organization.

street crime was the top priority for most Iraqis.[3] Meanwhile, the unstable security situation affected the operations and perceptions of foreign contractors working on Iraqi reconstruction; contributing to the CPA's failure to achieve key objectives, such as boosting electrical power output as rapidly as promised.[4]

These indicators are reinforced by the metric "transition to local control" used by CJTF-7 and MNF-I. During 2003, CJTF-7's expectation was that coalition forces would be able to transition to a situation in which Iraqi forces were preeminent in much of the country by spring 2004. In early 2004, CJTF-7 officially concluded that this process was likely to be set back by several months. The failures of ISF in April 2004 and the spikes in insurgent activity during summer of 2004 delayed this transition further still.

However, while the security outcomes have worsened since April 2003, we cannot conclude a great deal from this about the performance of the Iraqi security sector. Coalition forces have had primary responsibility for Iraqi internal security since the end of the war, so they must bear primary responsibility for any failures to restore order or to counter political violence. That said, the performance of Iraqi security forces under these conditions provide some, albeit caveated, insights. There have been notable failures of ISF, such as the desertions in Al-Anbar province and the south-central region in April 2004, and it is clear that the judicial and law enforcement institutions are "too easily intimidated."[5] However, during the intensive fighting against Jaish al-Mahdi in the summer of 2004, the IPS and ING performed much better than in April, indicating that they had become stronger institutions with more effective leadership in the meantime.

---

[3] Oxford Research International, *National Survey of Iraq*, June 2004; U.S. Department of State (2004).

[4] In July 2004, the U.S. administration reported to Congress that: "security problems have slowed reconstruction. Disruptions due to attacks and threats against drivers and vehicles have slowed the delivery of construction materials and supplies; attacks and threats have also been made against technical experts repairing, installing, and commissioning specialized equipment, particularly impacting the pace of power generation projects." *Quarterly Report to Congress* (2004).

[5] CPA, *Strategic Plan*, June 25, 2004.

The Iraqi Security Sector at Transition

By the time of the transfer of authority (June 28, 2004), the Iraqi security sector, outside Kurdistan, was unable to enforce the rule of law or to guarantee public safety. Whether assessed in terms of numbers of trained personnel, deployment of equipment, creation of infrastructure, unit operational capability, institutional development, command and control mechanisms, or governance arrangements, the capacity-building, reconstruction, and reform program was clearly in its early stages. More broadly, efforts to ensure the rule of law by removing corruption and organized crime from the body politic were in their infancy.

To some extent, this was to be expected. In other cases of SSR in post-conflict and transitional states, making a real difference requires many years of sustained investment by the international community as well as top-level commitment from the host state.[6] However, in few other cases has the United States or the international community sought to undertake such a thoroughgoing reconstruction and reform program in the face of such severe levels of violence.[7]

Below we summarize the state of the elements of the Iraqi security sector at transition, note developments since transition, and highlight key outstanding issues in each area.

National Security Institutions

The Ministerial Committee on National Security, known also as the Supreme (or Higher) Security Committee, appeared to be functioning. However, the committee has been little more than a mechanism to bring key ministers together. Important as this function is, there is little sign yet of the development of true, regular coordination between ministries at the working level, facilitated by a national secu-

---

[6] Alan Bryden, "Understanding Security Sector Reform and Reconstruction," in Bryden and Hänggi (2004), pp. 259–275.

[7] Somalia is perhaps the most comparable case for which the international community had very ambitious objectives and faced a very challenging security environment.

rity advisory staff.[8] It was not until the end of summer 2004 that Prime Minister Allawi decided to supplant the CPA-appointed national security advisor with his own choice, Qasem Daoud.[9] The transition to the Iraqi Transitional Government after the January 2005 elections has led to a new constellation of forces around this post. Sustained international support for capacity-building will be important to institutionalize the processes.

The reversion to hierarchical, patronage-based stovepipes is a real danger in Iraq and would reduce the quality of national security policymaking if it occurred. This clearly happened in the IIG, whose ministers had little sense of collective cabinet responsibility, and is likely to persist as coalition governments emerge from the January and December 2005 national elections. Institutionalization of decisionmaking processes can only go so far in papering over fundamental political divides.

The Defense Sector

The effort to create a defense ministry from scratch in less than half a year was, from the beginning, recognized as likely to produce a partial solution. The focus on recruiting good people, untainted by the past, was correct and may serve Iraq well if the MoD is permitted to mature into a well-established organization. However, the lack of time available to institutionalize key processes in the new ministry makes it uncertain whether this maturity will be achieved. There were efforts by the IIG to replace CPA-appointed officials and to substitute the principle of merit-based appointments with patron-client relationships.

The institutional weakness of the MoD is a particular problem because the IAF program, including the ING, is advancing rapidly under the stewardship of MNF-I. The armed forces will continue to benefit from a considerable investment of resources and mentoring by

---

[8] To date, much of the staff work supporting the IIG is undertaken by MNF-I officers.

[9] The hiatus over the summer during which time the CPA appointee, Mowaffeq al-Rubaie, was nominally in post but untrusted by the prime minister points to a CPA error in assuming that the NSA post could ever be apolitical.

MNF-I as they engage in internal security operations. While this is important to meet immediate security requirements, it poses two serious risks: (1) that the armed forces will grow rapidly into a powerful institution, only nominally governed by a weak civilian ministry, or (2) that they will become primarily an internal security force.[10]

The Interior Ministry

By July 2004, the IPS and DBE recruiting, training, equipping, and infrastructure-building programs were beginning to look in better shape than ever before. The start of specialist and leadership training was especially beneficial. With the continued injection of foreign funds, equipment, advice, and military support, the police and border forces should have considerable capability within two years. Delays in particular programs, such as the first-responder network and national identification systems,[11] will, however, curtail the effectiveness of these forces. Furthermore, there remain serious concerns in two areas. First is the ability of the IPS to deal with political violence and with serious organized crime. Capabilities that may need to be imported here are the kinds of judicial-police initiatives taken, for instance, by the Italian authorities against the mafia. Second, institutional development in the MoI is proceeding at a very slow pace. The MoI needs to be transformed from a bloated, inefficient, corrupt institution dedicated to preying on the public to one whose mission is to serve and protect the Iraqi public. This massive task is only just beginning.

Border, population, and weapons control programs are vital to the restoration of stability but are suffering from a lack of investment. The expansion and training of border security forces is on the right track, but they need to be supported by the appropriate population control, immigration, and weapons registration systems if they are to be truly effective.

---

[10] It is noticeable that the IIG put a lot of its effort into forming specialized counterinsurgency army units, the Iraqi Intervention Force.

[11] ID cards, passports, vetting, weapons permits.

Infrastructure Security

The bulk of the infrastructure security forces, the Facilities Protection Service, is minimally trained and has limited functions. The FPS's management by parent ministries remains of variable quality. However, some of the more professional infrastructure security forces are doing a better job of protecting the installations for which they are responsible. An important outstanding issue is the regulation of private security firms and the ability of the state to dispense with the services of tribal guards who often demand protection money for securing stretches of power lines, railroad tracks, and roads that pass through the territories they control.

The Justice Sector

Judicial reform had made considerable progress since April 2003. The completion of the infrastructure and security projects planned under the FY 2004 U.S. supplemental will substantially bolster the judiciary. In practice, however, the sector never received the support it deserved. Even in the spring of 2004, when CJTF-7 took over the police mission, CENTCOM shied away from adding the justice and prisons sector to its additional tasks.

A long-term program of institutional development and training is still required. It is also vital that combined judicial and law enforcement institutions are developed that can confidently tackle organized and violent crime. Furthermore, the wider anticorruption effort has only begun to take root, and there is no certainty it will succeed. Establishing and upholding humane standards of treatment in Iraq's prisons will take a lengthy commitment by Iraqi and international bodies. All these tasks will require the mobilization of large-scale resources by the wider international community, a mobilization that is not yet on the horizon.[12]

---

[12] The United Kingdom and the European Union plan additional assistance programs, but these are unlikely to have an impact until 2006 at the earliest.

The Intelligence Services

The failure to develop an integrated and coordinated Iraqi intelligence capacity ranks as one of the critical failures of the CPA effort. Although there was initial reluctance by the CPA to become involved in building the intelligence sector, given the terrible record of Iraq's intelligence services in the past, it should rapidly have been evident that an Iraqi-owned intelligence capability was critical to the success of both the counterinsurgency campaign and the fight against organized crime. While U.S. and UK intelligence personnel began to build an intelligence service early on, CPA involvement and oversight began far too late, as did the creation of intelligence structures in the MoI and MoD and the effort to integrate these into a coherent whole. At the time of transition, and more recently, this sector remains confused and stovepiped. Effective functional partnerships among agencies have not been constructed, and the Iraqi government lacks adequate processes and structures to coordinate its intelligence analysis and requirements. The failure to rapidly build up police intelligence to tackle insurgents and organized crime is perhaps the most glaring gap in Iraq's capabilities. The criminal intelligence assistance program, though valuable, initially focused on the transfer of technology, while the development of a police "Special Branch" remains moribund.

Disarmament, Demobilization, and Reintegration

A formal DDR process was not appropriate in Iraq because the armed forces had self-demobilized. While it remains debatable how much the formal dissolution of the army helped fuel armed opposition to the coalition, it is clear that the loss of status among former officers, the lack of jobs, and a plentiful supply of weaponry have been factors in fueling the insurgency. The coalition addressed these concerns with a stipend program and the appointment of "clean" former officers to the security forces and ministries. The lesson may be that, while demobilization was unnecessary and disarmament perhaps unfeasible, more resources should have been devoted to reintegration from the start of the occupation.

In relation to militias, the late start and limited staff and budget applied to the TR process made success unlikely from the start, even if the political circumstances had been more propitious. From February through June 2004, significant progress was made, but without ongoing support from either the IIG or the coalition nations, the TR effort was doomed to languish.

Assessing Progress

Based on the above sectoral assessment, we can make some tentative, qualitative generalizations about how much progress was made in the Iraqi security sector, using our three-part model outlined in Chapter One. At the level of individuals, the coalition did make a major effort to remove Saddam-era officers and senior officials steeped in the abusive and corrupt ways of the old regime. These individuals would otherwise have been a brake on reform, as has indeed happened in the MoI. The coalition had some success in informing Iraqi political leaders and senior officials about the principles of good security sector governance; to varying degrees, these principles were passed on in the plethora of training courses for security force and civil service personnel.

The bulk of the coalition's SSR work concentrated on building effective security sector institutions, notably the ministries. The focus was on building their managerial and administrative capacity, but efforts were also made to inculcate reformed practices. There is a striking difference, for instance, between the MoD—rebuilt from scratch along U.S. and UK lines—and the MoI, which has been only marginally touched by efforts to develop it into an accountable and effective governance institution. Institutional reform has therefore been patchy but in any case is a very long-term process that will only succeed if future Iraqi leaderships champion the cause.

Integration across the security sector and with the wider society is also a mixed story. The Ministerial Committee on National Security and, to some extent, local-level joint coordination centers were partial success stories. The coalition, however, failed to overcome the rigid ministerial compartmentalization inherited from Saddam, and political factionalization under the IIG did little to ameliorate the situation. As for wider integration with society, the CPA and its successor Iraqi government did make some progress in reorienting the security sector into one that serves society rather than one that preys on it. The respect accorded the IPS and the IAF in opinion polls is striking, despite stories of rampant corruption and brutality among the police.[13]

Thus, although the security sector capacity-building and reform program was behind in many of its targets, in the longer view it was moving in the right direction and laying the foundations of what is likely to remain for some years a tremendously ambitious reconstruction and reform program. Just as it will take many years to rebuild and reform the capacity of the Iraqi state for civil governance at national and local levels, it will likely take many years to build anything approaching an effective and accountable security sector.

Broader Lessons from the CPA's Experience

Affecting each of the elements of Iraq's security sector were six broader underlying problems with the coalition's approach to security sector reform in Iraq, some of which are familiar from other nation-building operations. Understanding these problems provides important lessons both for the shape of the ongoing SSR effort in Iraq and for U.S. and allied SSR efforts in other post-conflict countries.

Worst-Case and Contingency Planning

Both during the run-up to the war and during the occupation, there was a reluctance among U.S. policymakers to conduct worst-case analysis. This had two effects: (1) a systematic underestimation of the task, costs, and time required to reconstruct and reform the Iraqi security sector, and (2) a failure to undertake contingency planning.

---

[13] Julian Borger, "US State Department Slams Iraqi Government's Human Rights Record," *Guardian*, March 2, 2005.

Before the war, this can be seen in the decision to assume a postwar scenario in which the Iraqi police ensured order and in which insurgent resistance was minimal. During the occupation, there was reluctance to examine the consequences of failures in existing plans. For instance, although intelligence community assessments did posit a worsening of insurgent violence through 2004, CPA planners did not assess the consequences of the failure to meet publicly announced targets, such as the rollout of ISF, withdrawals of coalition forces, or achievement of targets for reconstruction such as power generation.

Structural Constraints on Rational Policy Development

At the outset, the CPA had sought to adopt an integrated approach to the development of the Iraqi security sector,[14] but this approach rapidly unraveled.[15] For many reasons, it proved inordinately difficult to create a unified effort toward the development and implementation of policy on Iraqi SSR. One reason was the lack of a clear lead for the effort, with responsibility distributed among the CPA (and among different offices in the authority), CJTF-7, and the CIA—to say nothing of the involvement of agencies and departments in national capitals, particularly Washington. Another reason was the "tyranny of the immediate." The lack of prior preparation for the events that unfolded in Iraq during 2003 and 2004 meant that the CPA and CJTF-7, along with the national capitals, found themselves focused on crisis management rather than implementing long-term strategies. This "tyranny of the immediate" also meant that short-term fixes to immediate problems were developed without detailed consideration of the longer-term implications.[16]

A broader aspect of the relative disunity of command was the struggle to integrate security sector development with other elements

---

[14] Although throughout the life of the CPA there was sometimes a reluctance to consider the justice sector as part of the security sector.

[15] Coordination and "joined-up" policymaking within the coalition improved somewhat in 2004 with the creation of a new management structure reporting to Ambassador Bremer and the wider remit given to the new OSA director, David Gompert.

[16] For example, the "30k in 30 days" initiative and the expansion of the ICDC.

of the military campaign and the reconstruction effort. Coordination mechanisms were established at senior and working levels,[17] but these were often rough and ready.[18]

Mobilization of Funding and Personnel Inputs from Home Countries

In most nation-building operations, the mobilization of nonmilitary resources has been problematic. It takes time to recruit and deploy civilian administrators, notably police and justice advisors, to establish management structures, to raise and spend funds, and to acquire and deploy equipment. The U.S. government and other members of the international community became better at this mobilization through their experience of nation-building in the 1990s (e.g., Haiti, Bosnia, Kosovo, East Timor, Sierra Leone).[19]

In Iraq, the Bush administration's intention was that a unified chain of command reaching back to the Defense Department would make it easier to mobilize U.S. government resources. However, this proved not to be the case. The Defense Department still needed to rely on other departments, and it was often unable to mobilize the resources that the CPA had identified as necessary for key tasks. Manning for the CPA was a particular problem. It hovered just above 50 percent of authorized levels at best, and the U.S. government had no way of directing civilian personnel with the right skills to deploy to Iraq. As a result, the entire effort was undertaken almost entirely with people who were in country for too short of time, working outside of their areas of expertise and often at levels of responsibility far above what they were accustomed to.

However, other civilian government departments with more experience of managing post-conflict operations did little better. The U.S. State and Justice Departments' police assistance program, for

---

[17] For example, the executive board and the joint planning group.

[18] The Overlapping Risk charts produced monthly by the policy planning office helped decisionmakers to visualize cross-cutting policy areas.

[19] Dobbins et al. (2003).

instance, were overwhelmed by the scale of the operation and by the poor security situation.

Balancing the Long-Term Goals of Institution-Building with the Short-Term Needs of Fielding Iraqi Security Forces

In the transition from authoritarian regimes, there is a dilemma between undertaking gradual reforms, which will involve leaving in power elites who have blood on their hands, and sweeping away the old to build from the ground up. In Iraq, this dilemma was exacerbated by the pressure to respond to immediate needs, making long-term reform, whether immediate or gradual, seem like a luxury. The coalition's initial inclination was for sweeping reform in the security sector. It dissolved the armed forces, believing a callback of the melted away structures and personnel would not be effective, as well as the defense ministry, intelligence and security organizations, and police internal security units.

This dilemma was made more acute by the short time frame under which the CPA found itself working after November 15, 2003, and by the continuing security vacuum, which coalition forces were ill equipped to fill. The effort to build structures that could serve Iraq well in the future continued to fall by the wayside in the need to respond to immediate requirements. A policy of sweeping reform had obvious ethical attractions and could perhaps have been justified if the CPA had remained in charge for the many years required to transform the security institutions in the way originally intended. Even a more gradual reform program would have required a long-term presence, to ensure that reforms became firmly rooted. However, the immediate needs of both the security situation and the deadlines created by the November 15 agreement meant that neither option could be implemented in full. The result was some effort directed at sweeping change, some at gradual change, and a great many policy choices taken to reflect the needs of the moment.

Ensuring Iraqi Ownership of the Reform Process

In all nation-building operations, international organizations experience a tension between working through indigenous institutions to reform them and importing wholesale external capacity to better manage the situation. The trade-off is usually between short-term results and more durable, locally owned institutions.[20] The CPA faced this dilemma acutely and, for the first half of its existence, solved it by importing foreign expertise to manage Iraqi government affairs, notably in the security arena. It was only after the November 15 agreement had set a (short) timeline for the transfer of authority that the CPA concentrated on developing Iraqi leadership and building Iraqi capacity. By the spring of 2004, the CPA was eagerly seeking to hand over authority and responsibility to Iraqi officials.

This approach meant that, although some of the institutions and programs had been well designed, by June 2004 there was patchy Iraqi ownership and limited capacity in the security sector institutions. Efforts to educate Iraqi interlocutors and instill in them a sense of the international best practice in SSR were fairly extensive in relation to the IGC and the MoD and more limited in relation to the MoI. It remains unclear how much impact this education had on the Iraqi leadership and officials.

The incipient nature of SSR in Iraq was recognized by the CPA, which undertook extensive planning to provide medium-term assistance to the Iraqi security ministries and ISF after its demise. This assistance was meant to involve technical and institutional development advice and mentoring as well as support for the build-out of ISF. Unfortunately, the failure to provide the planned-for institutional development and technical assistance, notably in the MoI[21] but also at the apex of government,[22] means that the IIG was left to some extent to fend for itself.

---

[20] Francis Fukuyama, *State-Building: Governance and World Order in the 21st Century*, Ithaca, N.Y.: Cornell University Press, 2004.

[21] Both the MoI advisory team and CPATT remained significantly understaffed during 2004.

[22] The civil government mechanisms around the cabinet, the presidency, and prime minister's office have received assistance from DFID, but the national security structures have had little help aside from that provided by coalition forces.

Clarifying Long-Term Security Relationships

When the November 15 agreement was concluded, the coalition's intention was to conclude a formal security agreement with the IGC that would establish the future security relationship with Iraq. It was unclear at this stage whether this meant a series of bilateral agreements or some sort of multilateral arrangement. In the event, it was decided to rely on the words contained in UN Security Council Resolution 1546 and a number of informal coordination mechanisms established between MNF-I and the IIG. These structures govern the relationship between sovereign Iraq and foreign military forces deployed on its soil and are underpinned by an implicit U.S. security guarantee to Iraq.

The matter of future formal security commitments remains open. While the IIG and the Transitional Government may be reluctant, for political reasons, to engage in formal treaty-making, the future size, role, and structure of Iraq's security sector are clearly dependent on the alliances that Iraq builds. Put simply, if the United States and its allies formally guarantee Iraq protection against external territorial aggression for the foreseeable future, then Iraq will require only a small military and can concentrate on building internal security institutions.

Conclusions and Prospects

The political and security future of Iraq remains very uncertain, and the country is likely to be plagued by high levels of political violence and crime for some years to come.[23] A reformed and effective Iraqi security sector is only one part of the answer to this problem. The evolution of the political landscape, the size and effectiveness of multinational forces, and the impact on Iraqi opinion of the economic and societal reconstruction effort will all play key roles, as will the attitudes of Iraq's neighbors. Nonetheless, a robust but accountable

---

[23] "U.S. Intelligence Offers Gloomy Outlook for Iraq," Reuters, September 16, 2004.

security sector is a necessary prerequisite for progress in these other areas.[24] In the short term, this security sector needs to provide Iraqis the confidence that the fear with which they lived under Saddam no longer need rule their lives.[25] In the longer term, it needs to enforce a rule of law that will not only ensure public safety but will support competent, honest governance and provide an environment conducive to the protection of property and private enterprise. These tasks may seem less urgent than containing the violence but will be of fundamental importance to the future of Iraq's political and economic development.

Since June 2004, Iraq's partners have directed additional resources and effort at building the capacity of the Iraqi security sector.[26] There is a risk, however, that much of this funding will be taken up in the renewed effort to expand numbers of front-line security force personnel. While it may be desirable, for instance, to expand total police numbers to 135,000, as was mandated by MNF-I in the fall of 2004, it will be more important to invest in the intangibles that cannot be so easily quantified. These include development of joint judicial and police investigatory capabilities, institutional development of national security institutions and the MoI, development of coordinated intelligence services, and sustained support to the justice sector, including anticorruption programs. At present, for instance, the Iraqi police do not lack funds or equipment but do lack the ability to manage and apply these resources in an effective manner.

More fundamentally, Iraqi leaders and their international advisors need to examine the longer-term implications of their short-term actions. For instance, on the military side, the focus on short-term

---

[24] "Vicious Cycle of Violence Undermining UN Efforts to Rebuild Iraq—Top Envoy," UN News Service, September 14, 2004.

[25] "Iraq: UN Envoy Says 'Climate of Fear' Remains Entrenched," *Radio Free Europe*, September 15, 2004. The intimidation of Iraqis associated with the IIG or the international community appears to have worsened significantly since the demise of the CPA.

[26] Marc Grossman, "New Priorities for U.S. Assistance Under the Iraq Relief and Reconstruction Fund (IRRF)," Under Secretary for Political Affairs on-the-record briefing Washington, D.C., September 14, 2004.

solutions has led to a program for the rapid development of a large military force dedicated to internal security tasks. Although the concept behind the ING is that it will transition into a smaller force once the "emergency" is over and it can no longer operate under the wing of large coalition forces, there is no realistic transition plan in place.

This points to perhaps the most significant need, which is for the Iraqi government at the highest levels to develop the capacity to make and implement security policy. A start was made during 2004 with the drafting of a national security strategy, but Iraq's leaders lack the institutional capacity to formulate and execute policy, to systematically examine options, and to plan for the longer term. Because the transitional government will be in place for only a year, it is unlikely that it will go very far in institutionalizing the necessary processes. Nonetheless, while working out their visions and strategies for the development of the security sector, the Iraqi leadership and their international advisors will have to raise their gaze beyond implementing the current programs and start to tackle some of the basic, unanswered questions surrounding the future of the sector.

These questions are essentially political. Throughout Iraq's history, the center has used the security sector to coerce the country's regions and communities. In the face of the current security crisis, Baghdad has sought to go down this route, for instance, by reasserting the power of the interior ministry over provincial governors and police chiefs. This recentralization of power is, however, taking place in an environment in which there are also strong centripetal tendencies, such as non-state militias and the fact that populations in both the north and south of Iraq have begun to work toward more-autonomous relations with the center.[27] If the twin perils of overcentralization and Balkanization are to be avoided, then Iraqi leaders need to give serious thought to questions of center-region relationships, state-society relationships, and the proportion of national resources allocated to security. Only by tackling these issues sooner rather than later can Iraq's leaders ensure that the security sector both

---

[27] "Iraqi South Threatens Secession," *Al Jazeera*, August 10, 2004, http://english.aljazeera.net.

copes with the current crisis and provides a firm foundation for a well-governed and democratic state. This will be an important item for the National Assembly to debate later this year.

Unfortunately, we need to be realistic about the likelihood of the Iraqi Transitional Government having the ability or vision to tackle these strategic issues. Not surprisingly, Iraqi ministers and senior officials are likely to be more focused in coming months on their personal positions, even survival, than on long-term institution-building.[28] The United States, the United Kingdom, and their international partners will have to work hard to ensure that long-term institution-building remains on the Iraqi agenda.

---

[28] The fact that the IIG's interior minister felt it necessary to build his own commando force rather than use the CPATT-designed CIF, which reported to a deputy minister whom he did not trust, highlights the approach many Iraqi leaders are likely to take over the coming months.

Bibliography

"Allawi Creates Iraq Anti-Terror Force," MSNBC News, July 15, 2004.

Barton, Rick, and Bathsheba Croker, *Progress or Peril? Measuring Iraq's Reconstruction*, Washington, D.C.: Center for Strategic and International Studies, September 2004.

Bayley, David H., *Patterns of Policing: A Comparative International Analysis*, New Brunswick, N.J.: Rutgers University Press, 1990.

Borger, Julian, "US State Department Slams Iraqi Government's Human Rights Record," *Guardian*, March 2, 2005.

Bremer, L. Paul, III, "What I Really Said About Iraq," *New York Times*, October 8, 2004.

Brookings Institution, Iraq Index, www.brookings.edu/iraqindex.

Bryden, Alan, and Heiner Hänggi, eds., *Reform and Reconstruction of the Security Sector*, Münster, Germany: Lit Verlag, 2004.

Burack, James, William Lewis, and Edward Marks, *Civilian Police and Multinational Peacekeeping—A Workshop Series: A Role for Democratic Policing*, Washington, D.C.: National Institute of Justice, October 6, 1997 (January 1999)

Coalition Provisional Authority, CPA Order 2, Dissolution of Entities with Annex A, May 23, 2003.

———, *Iraqi Police: An Assessment of the Present and Recommendations for the Future*, May 30, 2003.

———, CPA Order 26, Creation of the Department of Border Enforcement, August 24, 2003.

————, CPA Order 35, Re-establishment of the Council of Judges, September 15, 2003.

————, *Security Sector Synchronization Exercise Outbrief,* October 11, 2003.

————, *Ministry of Interior Organizational Plan,* November 2003.

————, *Iraq: Integrated Security Sector Development,* Office of Policy Planning, December 4, 2003.

————, *Framework for Iraqi National Security Institution Building,* December 10, 2003.

————, "Commission on Public Integrity to Combat Government Corruption," press release, January 31, 2004. Online at www.iraqCoalition. org/pressreleases/20040131_IGC_integrity_PR.html (as of June 2005).

————, CPA Order 57, Iraqi Inspectors General, February 10, 2004.

————, CPA Order 61, Amendment to Order 45, February 22, 2004.

————, CPA Order 71, Local Governmental Powers, April 6, 2004.

————, CPA Order 13, The Central Criminal Court of Iraq (Amended), April 22, 2004.

————, CPA Order 77, Board of Supreme Audit, April 25, 2004.

————, *Transition and Reintegration Strategy,* May 2004.

————, CPA Order 91, Regulation of Armed Forces and Militias Within Iraq, June 2004.

————, *Strategic Plan,* June 25, 2004.

————, *Security Sector Reform: An Example of Structures Designed for Counter-Insurgency and for the Transition,* November 29, 2004.

Cordesman, Anthony H., *Inexcusable Failure: Progress in Training the Iraqi Army and Security Forces as of Mid-July 2004,* Washington, D.C.: Center for Strategic and International Studies, July 20, 2004.

————, *Strengthening Iraqi Military and Security Forces,* Washington, D.C.: Center for Strategic and International Studies, January 28, 2005.

Dahrendorf, Nicola, ed., *A Review of Peace Operations: A Case for Change,* London: King's College London, 2003.

Dobbins, James, John G. McGinn, Keith Crane, Seth G. Jones, Rollie Lal, Andrew Rathmell, Rachel Swanger, and Anga Timilsina, *America's Role in Nation-Building: From Germany to Iraq*, Santa Monica, Calif.: RAND Corporation, MR-1753-RC, 2003.

Fallows, James, "Blind into Baghdad," *The Atlantic Monthly*, January/February 2004.

Fineman, Mark, "Arms Plan for Iraqi Forces Is Questioned," *Los Angeles Times*, August 8, 2003.

Fukuyama, Francis, *State-Building: Governance and World Order in the 21st Century*, Ithaca, N.Y.: Cornell University Press, 2004.

Gompert, David C., Olga Oliker, and Anga Timilsina, *Clean, Lean, and Able: A Strategy for Defense Development*, Santa Monica, Calif.: RAND Corporation, OP-101-RC, 2004.

Grossman, Marc, "New Priorities for U.S. Assistance Under the Iraq Relief and Reconstruction Fund (IRRF)," Under Secretary for Political Affairs on-the-record briefing, Washington, D.C., September 14, 2004.

Hänggi, Heiner, "Conceptualising Security Sector Reform and Reconstruction," in Bryden and Hänggi (2004).

Hansen, Annika S., *From Congo to Kosovo: Civilian Police in Peace Operations*, Adelphi Paper 343, London: International Institute for Strategic Studies, 2002.

Hess, Pamela, "DOD, State Need Billions for Iraq," United Press International, April 21, 2004.

Hodge, Nathan, "Northrop Grumman to Train New Iraqi Army," *Jane's Defence Weekly*, July 7, 2003.

———, "Pentagon Agency May Train Iraqi War-Crimes Prosecutors," *Jane's Defence Weekly*, September 15, 2003.

Hosmer, Stephen T., and Olga Oliker, *Countering Insurgency in Iraq: Improving Security Policies and Instruments*, Santa Monica, Calif.: RAND Corporation, forthcoming.

Hyden, Goran, Julius Court, and Kenneth Mease, *Making Sense of Governance*, Boulder, Colo.: Lynne Rienner, 2004.

International Republican Institute, *Survey of Iraqi Public Opinion, December 26, 2004–January 7, 2005*, Washington, D.C., 2005.

Iraq Body Count Project, www.iraqbodycount.org.

Iraq Coalition Casualty Count, http://icasualties.org/oif.

"Iraq: UN Envoy Says 'Climate of Fear' Remains Entrenched," *Radio Free Europe*, September 15, 2004.

Iraqi Ministry of Defense, *2005 Defense Plan*, draft, December 1, 2004.

Iraqi National Intelligence Service Charter, issued by Iraq's Governing Council, April 2, 2004.

"Iraqi South Threatens Secession," *Al Jazeera*, August 10, 2004, http://english.aljazeera.net.

Jaffe, Greg, "New Factor in Iraq: Irregular Brigades Fill Security Void," *Wall Street Journal*, February 16, 2005.

Jones, Seth G., Jeremy M. Wilson, Andrew Rathmell, and K. Jack Riley, *Establishing Law and Order After Conflict*, Santa Monica, Calif.: RAND Corporation, MG-374-RC, 2005.

Oakley, Robert B., Michael J. Dziedzic, and Eliot M. Goldberg, eds., *Policing the New World Disorder: Peace Operations and Public Security*, Washington, D.C.: National Defense University, 1998.

Organisation for Economic Co-operation and Development, *Security System Reform: Policy and Good Practice*, Development Assistance Committee, Network on Conflict, Peace and Development Co-operation October 1, 2003.

Oxford Research International, *National Survey of Iraq*, June 2004.

Perito, Robert M., *Where Is the Lone Ranger When We Need Him? America's Search for a Postconflict Stability Force*, Washington, D.C.: United States Institute of Peace, 2004.

Quarterly Report to Congress, 2207 report, July 2004.

Rathmell, Andrew, "Building Counterterrorism Strategies and Institutions: The Iraqi Experience," presentation to RAND conference, "Three Years After: Next Steps in the War on Terror," Washington, D.C., September 8, 2004.

Ronco Corporation, "Decision Brief to Department of Defense Office of Reconstruction and Humanitarian Assistance on the Disarmament, Demobilization and Reintegration of the Iraqi Armed Forces," March 2003.

Shanker, Thom, "US Is Speeding Up Plans for Creating a New Iraqi Army," *New York Times*, September 18, 2003.

Slocombe, Walter B., "Iraq's Special Challenge: Security Sector Reform 'Under Fire'," in Bryden and Hänggi 2004.

UK Department for International Development, *Understanding and Supporting Security Sector Reform,* London, undated.

UK House of Commons Defence Committee, *Evidence of Mr Martin Howard, Lt General John McColl, Major General Nick Houghton and Major General Bill Rollo,* HC 65-ii, January 6, 2005.

———, *Oral Evidence of Dr Owen Greene, Chief Constable Paul Kernaghan, Mr Stephen Pattison and Mr Stephen Rimmer,* HC 65-I, January 26, 2005.

U.S. Department of State, *Opinion Analysis,* M-71-04, June 17, 2004.

———, *Fear a Key Factor on Iraqi Political Outlook*, Opinion Analysis, Office of Research, January 18, 2005.

"U.S. Intelligence Offers Gloomy Outlook for Iraq," Reuters, September 16, 2004.

"Vicious Cycle of Violence Undermining UN Efforts to Rebuild Iraq—Top Envoy," UN News Service, September 14, 2004.

World Bank, Governance Indicators, 1996–2004, 2005, www.worldbank.org/wbi/governance/govdata2002/ (as of June 2005).